AF594820

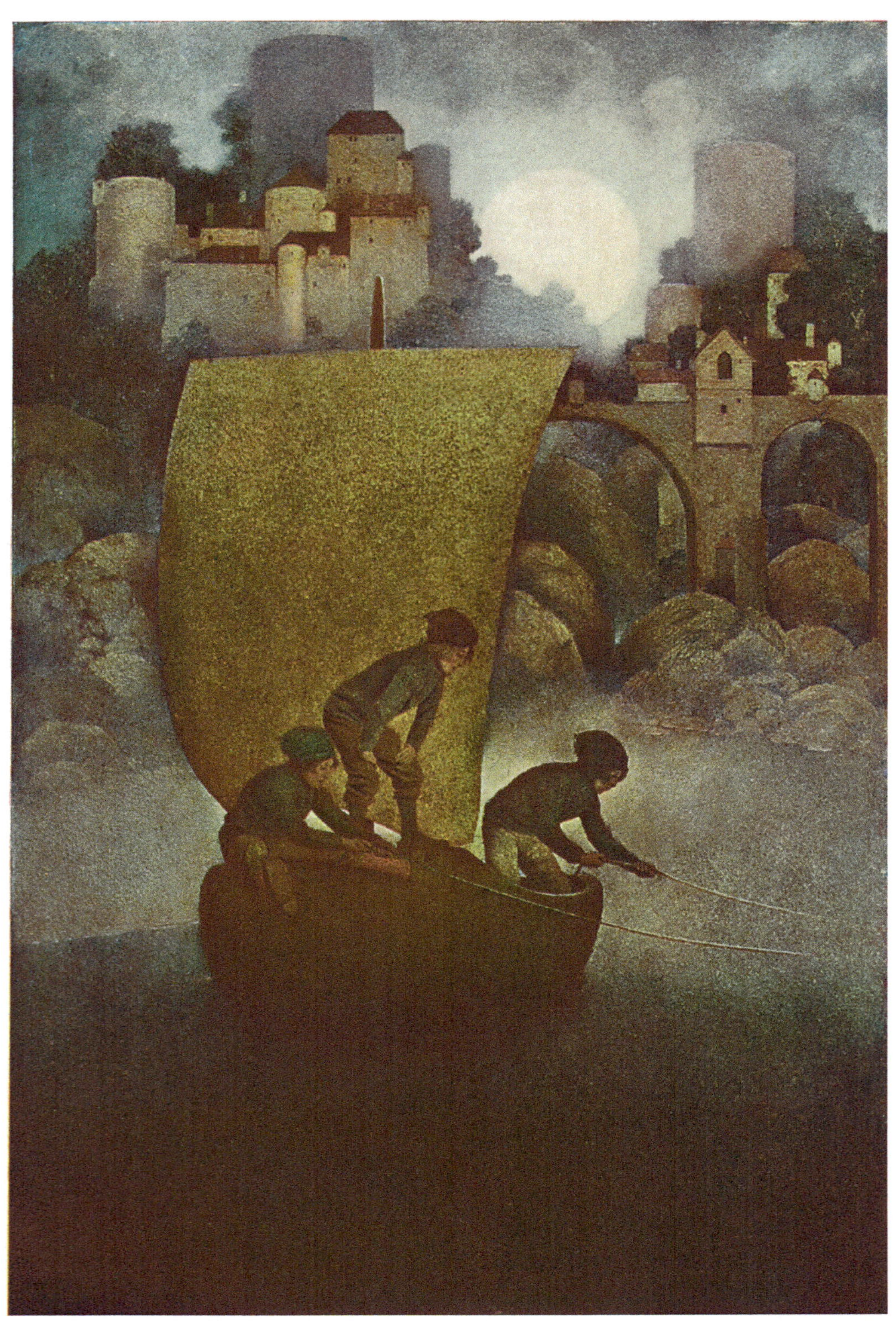

"Wynken, Blynken and Nod"

Wynken, Blynken and Nod one night
Sailed off in a wooden shoe—
Sailed on a river of crystal light,
Into a sea of dew
Poems of Childhood, 1904

Worlds of Enchantment

THE ART OF Maxfield Parrish

Selected and Edited by Jeff A. Menges

DOVER PUBLICATIONS
Garden City, New York

Copyright

Bibliographical Note

This Dover edition, first published in 2010, is an original compilation of illustrations from the following list of sources (arranged in chronological order): *Century Magazine* (1896; December 1898; December 1901; 1902); The Mask and Wig Club (1898); *Scribner's Magazine* (April 1899; October 1899; August 1912); *The Golden Age* by Kenneth Grahame (John Lane: The Bodley Head, London and New York, 1900); *Knickerbocker's History of New York* by Washington Irving (R. H. Russell, New York, 1900); *Success* magazine (December 1901); *Dream Days* by Kenneth Grahame (John Lane: The Bodley Head, London and New York, 1902); "Italian Villas and Their Gardens" by Edith Wharton (*Century Magazine,* November 1904); *Ladies' Home Journal* (1904); *Poems of Childhood* by Eugene Field (Charles Scribner's Sons, New York, 1904); *The Arabian Nights: Their Best-Known Tales,* edited by Kate Douglas Wiggin and Nora A. Smith (Charles Scribner's Sons, New York, 1909); *Collier's* magazine (July 30, 1910); *Tanglewood Tales* from *A Wonder Book and Tanglewood Tales* by Nathaniel Hawthorne (Duffield & Company, New York, 1910); *The Golden Treasury of Songs and Lyrics* by Francis Turner Palgrave (Duffield & Company, New York, 1911); *Hearst* magazine (August 1912; November 1912); The Curtis Publishing Company (1912–1915); Edison Mazda Lamps Calendars (1918–21; 1923–24; 1926–27; 1929–31); House of Art (1918; 1922; 1926); The Memorial Library of the University of Rochester (1922); *Life* magazine (April 1922); and *The Knave of Hearts* by Louise Saunders (Charles Scribner and Sons, New York, 1925).

Library of Congress Cataloging-in-Publication Data

Parrish, Maxfield, 1870–1966.
Worlds of enchantment : the art of Maxfield Parrish / selected and edited by Jeff A. Menges. — Dover ed.
p. cm.
Original compilation of illustrations from a variety of sources published between 1896 and 1926.
ISBN-13: 978-0-486-47306-2
ISBN-10: 0-486-47306-6
1. Parrish, Maxfield, 1870–1966—Themes, motives. I. Menges, Jeff A. II. Title. III. Title: Art of Maxfield Parrish.

NC975.5.P37A4 2010
759.13—dc22

2009046016

Printed in Canada
47306612 2025
www.doverpublications.com

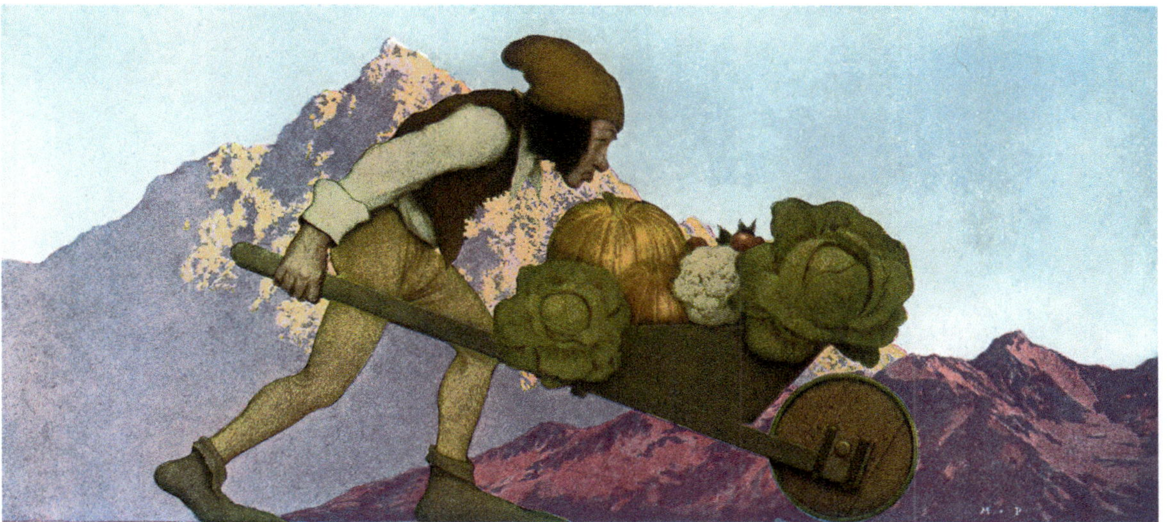

Barrow with Vegetables, *The Knave of Hearts*, 1925

Introduction

Maxfield Parrish stands some distance apart from his contemporary illustrators of the twentieth century. His long and productive career covered nearly two-thirds of the last century, and it would be hard to find another artist who could be called more successful in the visual arts. Forty years of highly specialized commercial illustration work, followed by another thirty years of very personal introspective work, created a legacy, and a unique "look," that continues to be extremely popular, as well as being the exclusive property of one artist—Maxfield Parrish.

He was born Frederick Maxfield Parrish in 1870 in Philadelphia, Pennsylvania. As a young boy he was encouraged by a father who was always interested in art. Both of Frederick's parents were supportive of his creative expression, and young Parrish was given many opportunities to exercise it. When he was in his mid-teens, the family went traveling through Europe; there, Frederick got a first-hand look at the works of the Renaissance masters, the Impressionists, and the Pre-Raphaelites.

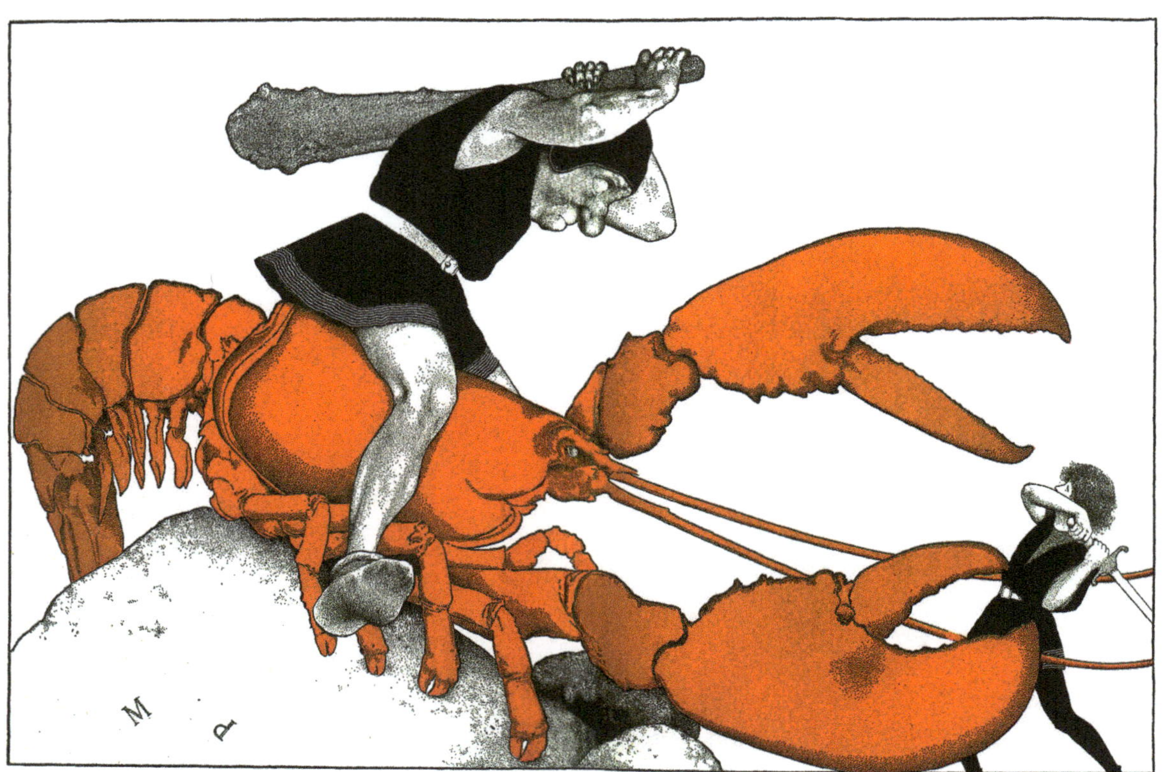

Endpaper from 1904

After nearly two years in Europe, the Parrishes returned to the Philadelphia area. Soon Frederick enrolled at Haverford College (1888), where his interest in design and architecture led him to pursue that course of study, but art was where he excelled, and it eventually won him over. After Haverford, in 1892, Parrish enrolled at the Pennsylvania Academy of Fine Arts. A year later he crossed paths with another giant of early American illustration, Howard Pyle. Parrish was still looking for his path, but Pyle could recognize that he had all the tools he needed, and he told Parrish as much. Frederick audited a few of Pyle's classes, and then went on to prove himself. In 1894 Parrish began to receive steady commercial work, and for the next four years he ran a small studio in downtown Philadelphia and further developed his style. He also adopted his middle name—*Maxfield,* a family name—for his identity in commercial work.

Parrish's early style was strong and bold, accented with a dash of humor. It served him very well in the magazine market, where he became a regular contributor to *Collier's, Scribner's,* and the *Harper's* family of publications, among the many popular periodicals of the time. His characters were so playful and humorous that his artistry seemed a perfect fit for the appropriate children's book, and, in 1897, *Mother Goose in Prose*—both Parrish's first illustrated book and the first book by Frank Baum (of *Oz* fame)—found its way from Parrish's studio to the bookstores.

In 1898 Parrish and his wife, Lydia, relocated. Illustration work was brisk, but Parrish desired a place in the country in order to work undisturbed, and he found it in Cornish, New Hampshire. Many artists and writers had settled in the area, establishing a colony of sorts. The locale agreed greatly with Parrish, and it was a constant source of inspiration for the rest of his life. More magazine work, an occasional book assignment, and some lucrative advertising work provided the general rotation of tasks in Parrish's studio for most of his working years.

Poems of Childhood by Eugene Field was the first book to feature Parrish's paintings in *full* color. This success was followed by a lengthy magazine assignment in a very different area, featuring his illustrations for "Italian Gardens and their Villas" by Edith Wharton, appearing in *Century* magazine in 1904. These two assignments served as bookends in defining the type of work Parrish would devote himself to for the next twenty-five years: the first, the humorous characters for which he became so well known, and the second, architecture and landscape, passions that would occupy the last quarter-century of Parrish's life.

In this new selection of images, we look at Parrish's commercial years, from early magazine pieces through the prints and advertising work that brought him fame, and up to his last color book work, what many consider to be his greatest collected work, *The Knave of Hearts.*

Jeff A. Menges
July 2009

List of Plates

DREAM DAYS by Kenneth Grahame, illustrated by Maxfield Parrish (John Lane: The Bodley Head, London and New York, 1902)

17. The Reluctant Dragon
18. Dies Irae
19. A Saga of the Seas
20. The Twenty-first of October

ITALIAN VILLAS AND THEIR GARDENS by Edith Wharton, with pictures by Maxfield Parrish (*Century Magazine,* November 1904)

21. Villa Gamberaia, near Florence
22. Vicobello, Siena
23. La Palazzina [Villa Gori], Siena
24. Villa Scassi, Genoa
25. In the Gardens of Isola Bella, Lake Maggiore
26. Villa Torlonia, Rome

LADIES' HOME JOURNAL, 1904

27. Cover, "Air Castles"

POEMS OF CHILDHOOD

28. "With Trumpet and Drum." With big tin trumpet and little red drum,/ Marching like soldiers, the children come!
29. "The Sugar-Plum Tree." And you carry away of the treasure that rains/ As much as your apron can hold!
30. "The Little Peach." John took a bite and Sue a chew,/And then the trouble began to brew,—/ Trouble the doctor couldn't subdue./Too true!
31. "The Dinkey-Bird." In an ocean, 'way out yonder/(As all sapient people know),/Is the land of Wonder-Wander,/Whither children love to go.
32. "Shuffle-Shoon and Amber-Locks." Shuffle-Shoon and Amber-Locks/ Sit together, building blocks;/Shuffle-Shoon is old and gray,/ Amber-Locks is a little child.
33. "Seein' Things." I woke up in the dark an' saw things standin' in a row,/ A-lookin' at me cross-eyed an' p'intin' at me—so!

SCRIBNER'S Magazine, August 1912

34. The Land of Make-Believe [painted in 1905]

COLLIER'S Magazine, December 12, 1908

35. Cover

THE ARABIAN NIGHTS: THEIR BEST-KNOWN TALES, edited by Kate Douglas Wiggin and Nora A. Smith, illustrated by Maxfield Parrish [Charles Scribner's Sons, New York, 1909]

36. Sinbad Plots against the Giant
37. Gulnare of the Sea
38. The Young King of the Black Isles
39. The Story of the King's Son
40. Cassim in the Cave of the Forty Thieves
41. The History of Codadad and His Brothers

COLLIER'S Magazine, July 30, 1910

42. Cover

TANGLEWOOD TALES [*A Wonder Book and Tanglewood Tales*] by Nathaniel Hawthorne, illustrated by Maxfield Parrish (Duffield & Company, New York, 1910)

43. Jason and the Talking Oak
44. Pandora
45. Atlas
46. Cadmus Sowing the Dragon's Teeth
47. Jason and His Teacher

THE GOLDEN TREASURY OF SONGS AND LYRICS by Francis Turner Palgrave, illustrated by Maxfield Parrish (Duffield & Company, New York, 1911)

48. Harvest
49. The Lantern Bearers
50. Summer
51. Autumn
52. Pierrot
53. Easter

HEARST'S Magazine

54. Cover, "The Story of Snow Drop," August 1912
55. Cover, "The Sleeping Beauty," November 1912

THE CURTIS PUBLISHING COMPANY, 1912–1915

56. Mural panel
57. Mural panel

EDISON MAZDA LAMPS CALENDAR

58. *Cinderella* aka *Enchantment*, 1926

FLORENTINE FETE

59. Mural, 1916

EDISON MAZDA LAMPS CALENDAR

60. *And the Night Is Fled*, 1918

HOUSE OF ART

61. Print, "Garden of Allah,"1918

SWIFT'S PREMIUM

62. *Jack Sprat*, Swift's Premium Ham Advertisement, 1919

EDISON MAZDA LAMPS CALENDAR

63. *Spirit of the Night*, 1919
64. *Prometheus*, 1920
65. *Egypt*, 1922

FERRY'S SEEDS

66. Advertisement, 1921

JELL-O

67. Advertisement, "King and Queen," 1921
    Advertisement, "Polly put the Kettle on," 1921

HOUSE OF ART

68. Print, "Daybreak," 1922

THE MEMORIAL ART GALLERY OF THE UNIVERSITY OF ROCHESTER

69. Mural, *Interlude,* 1922

LIFE Magazine

70. Cover, "Morning," April 1922

EDISON MAZDA LAMPS CALENDAR

71. *The Lamp Seller of Bag[h]dad,* 1923
72. *Venetian Lamplighter,* 1924

THE KNAVE OF HEARTS

73. Bookplate: This Is the Book of
74. Frontispiece: Lady Violetta
75. Blue Hose/Yellow Hose
76. Lady Ursula kneeling before the King
77. The Knave
78. The Chancellor, the King, and Yellow Hose

HOUSE OF ART

79. Print, "Stars," 1926
80. Print, "Hilltop," 1926

EDISON MAZDA LAMPS CALENDAR

81. *Contentment,* 1928
82. *Ecstasy,* 1930
83. *Waterfall,* 1931
84. *Solitude,* 1932

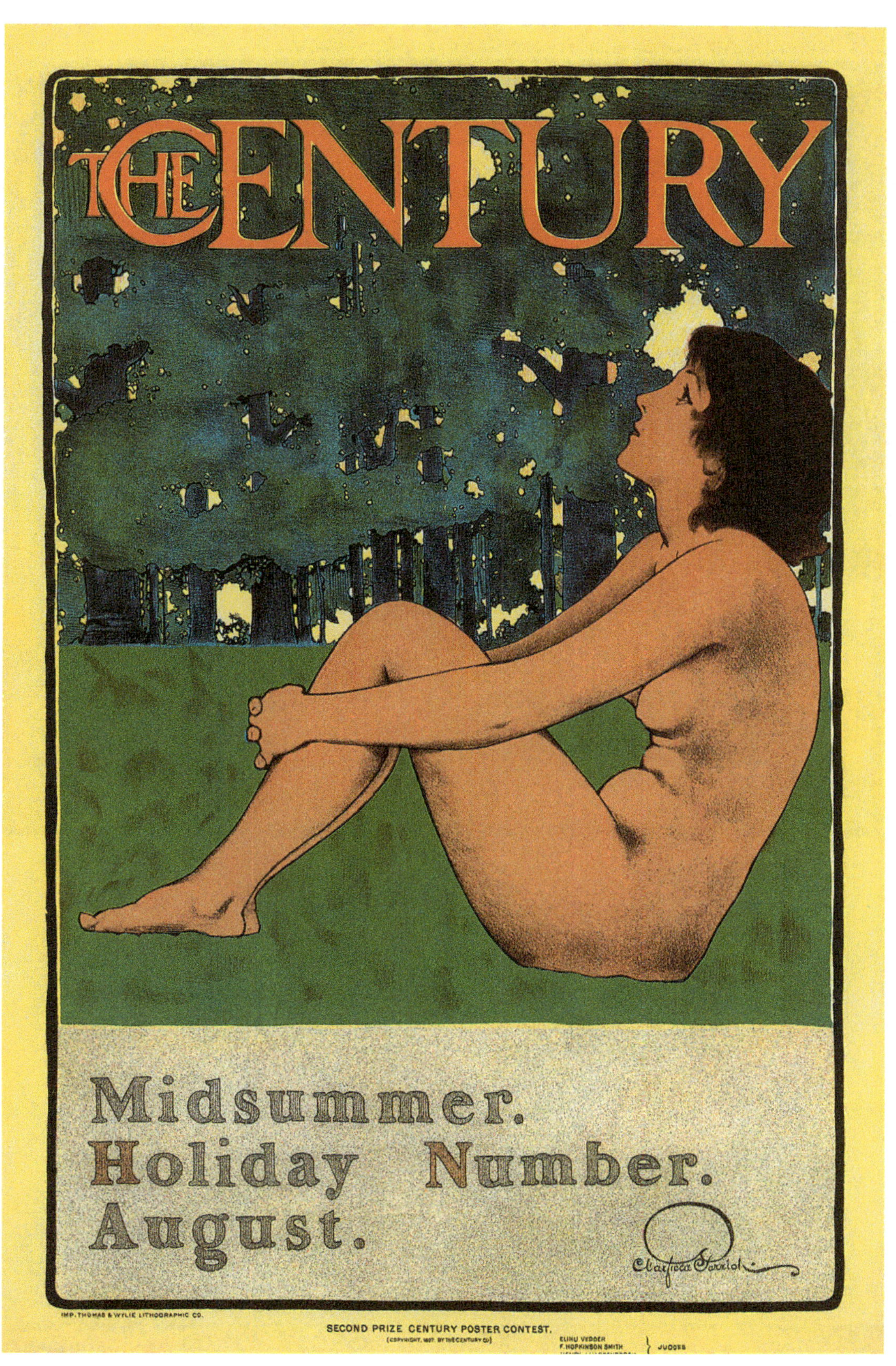

PLATE 1.

Second Prize
The Century Poster Contest, 1896

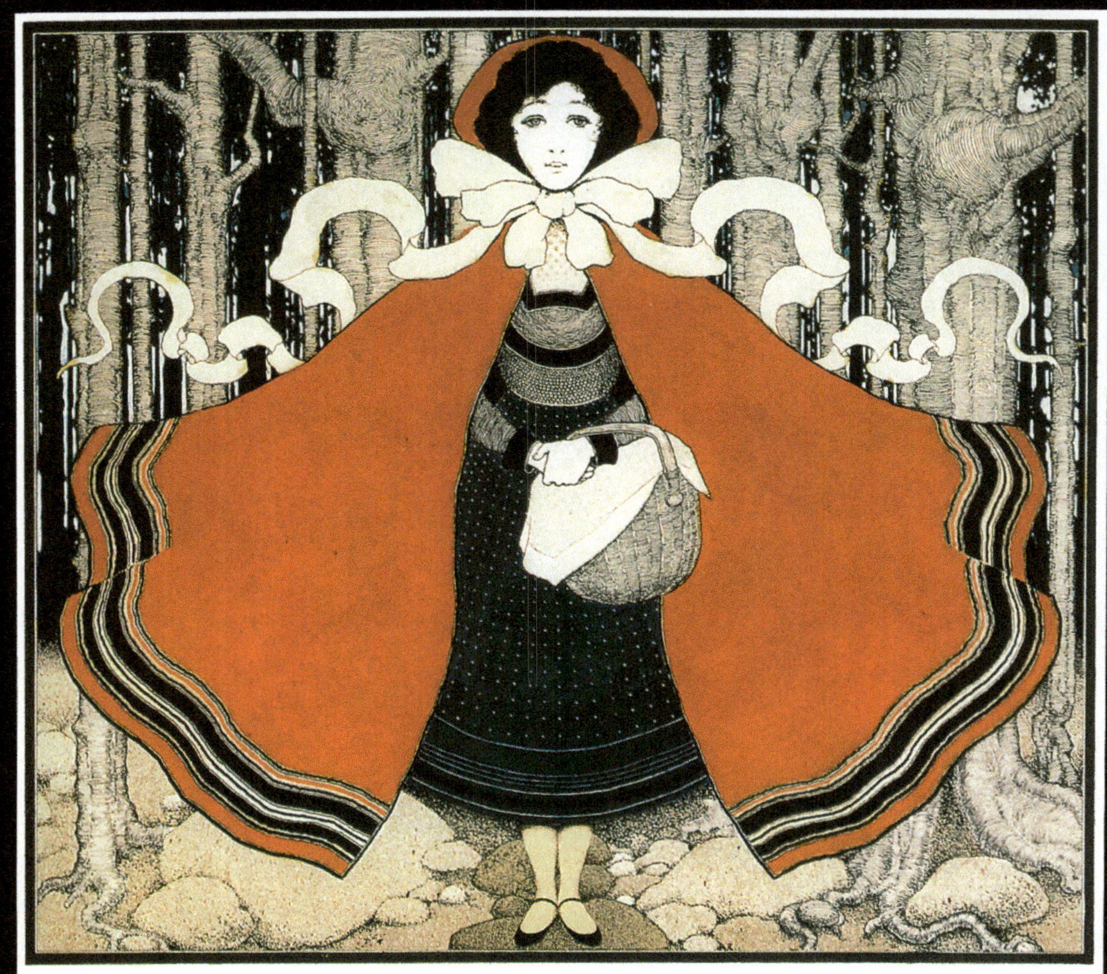

Plate 2.

Very Little Red Riding Hood
The Mask and Wig Club, 1898

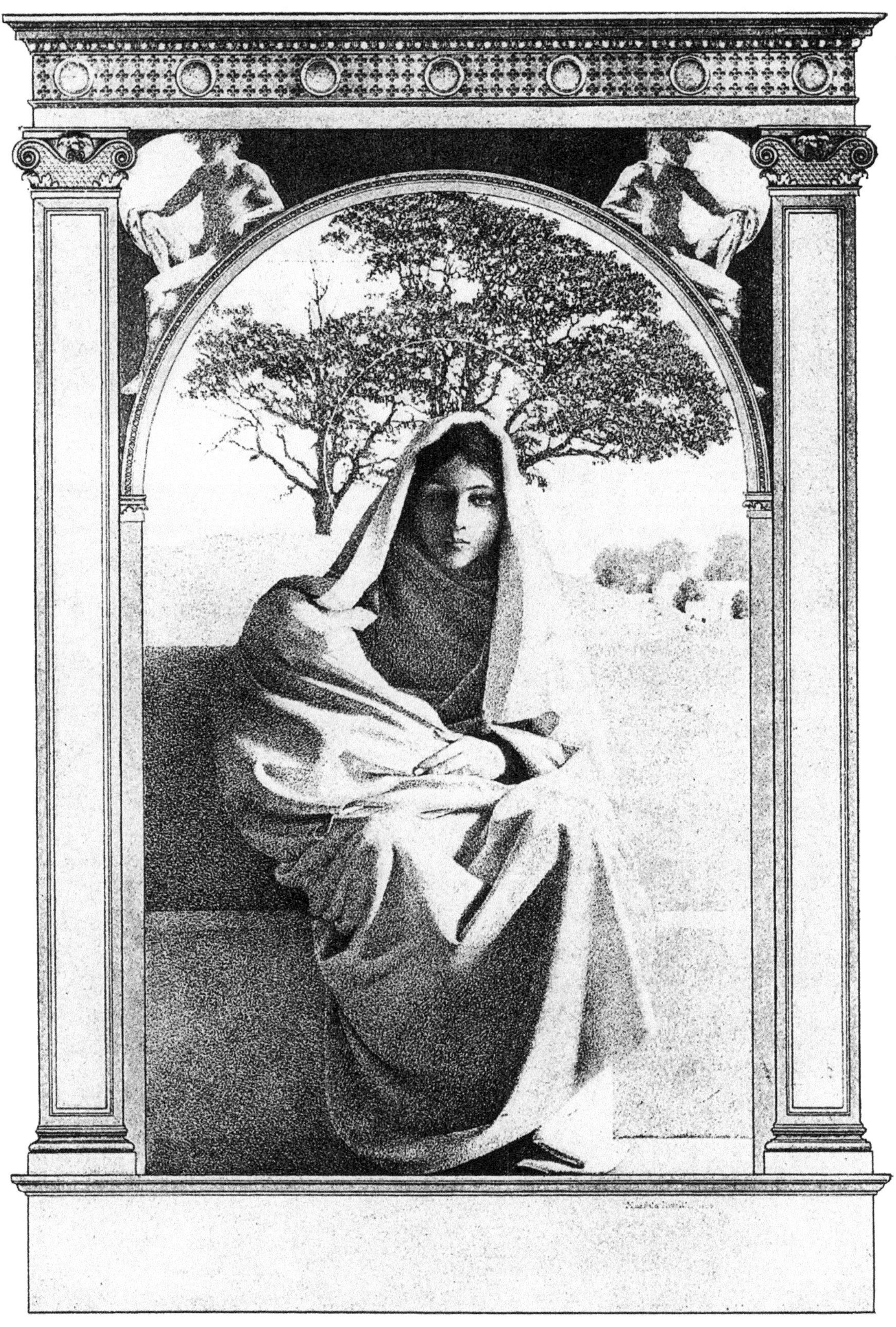

Plate 3.

Christmas Eve
Century Magazine, December 1898

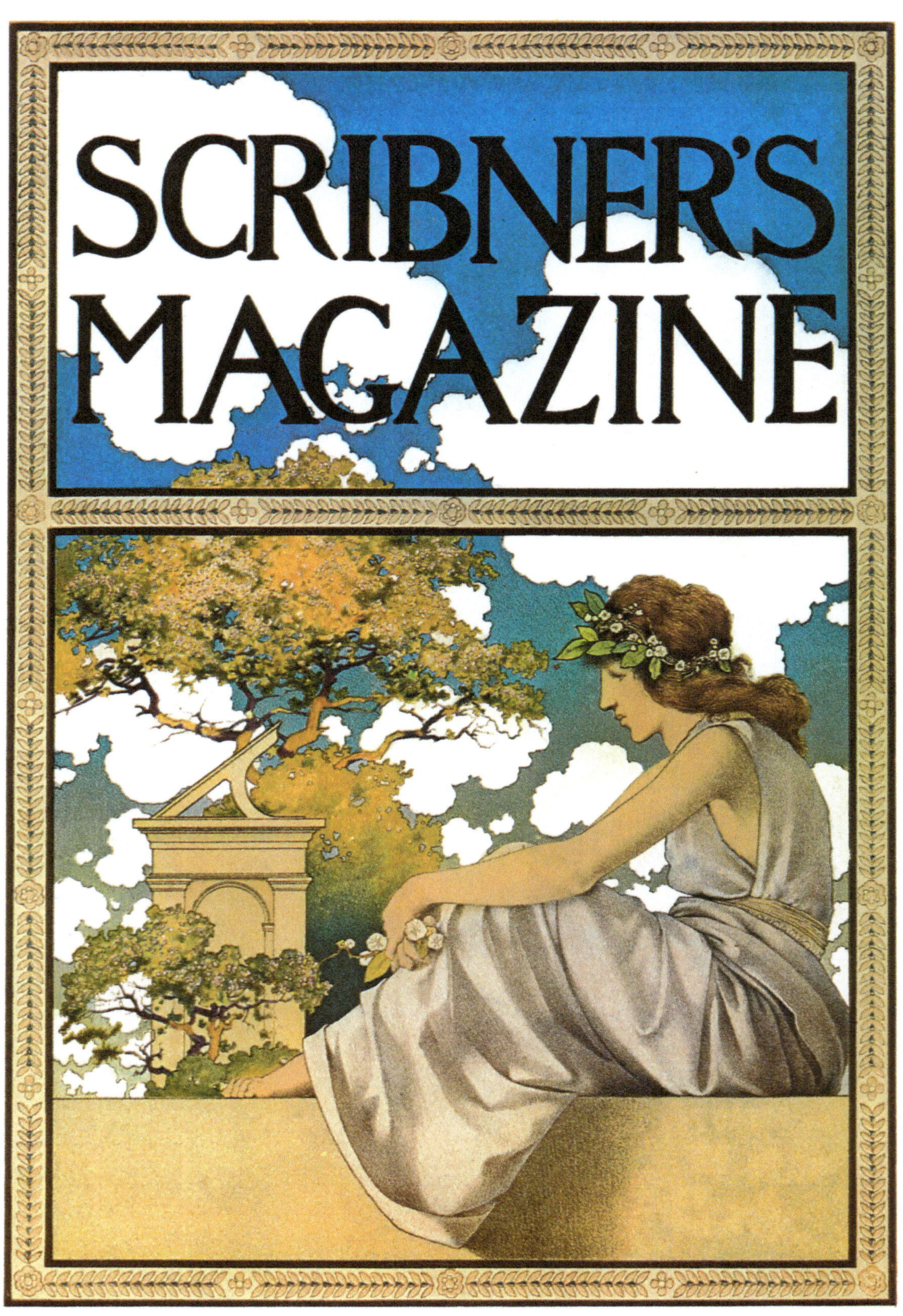

Plate 4.

Cover
Scribner's Magazine, April 1899

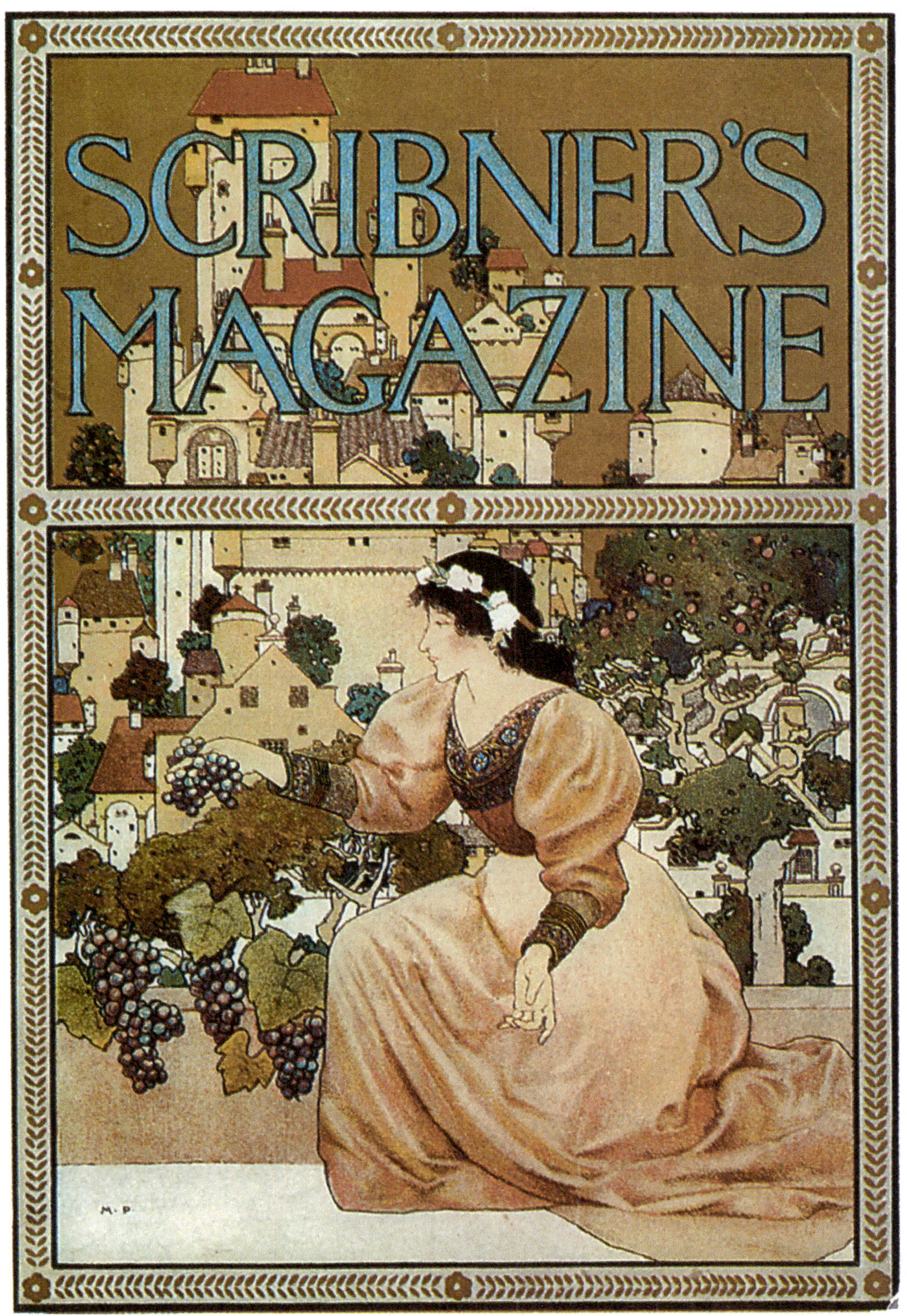

Plate 5.

Cover
Scribner's Magazine, October 1899

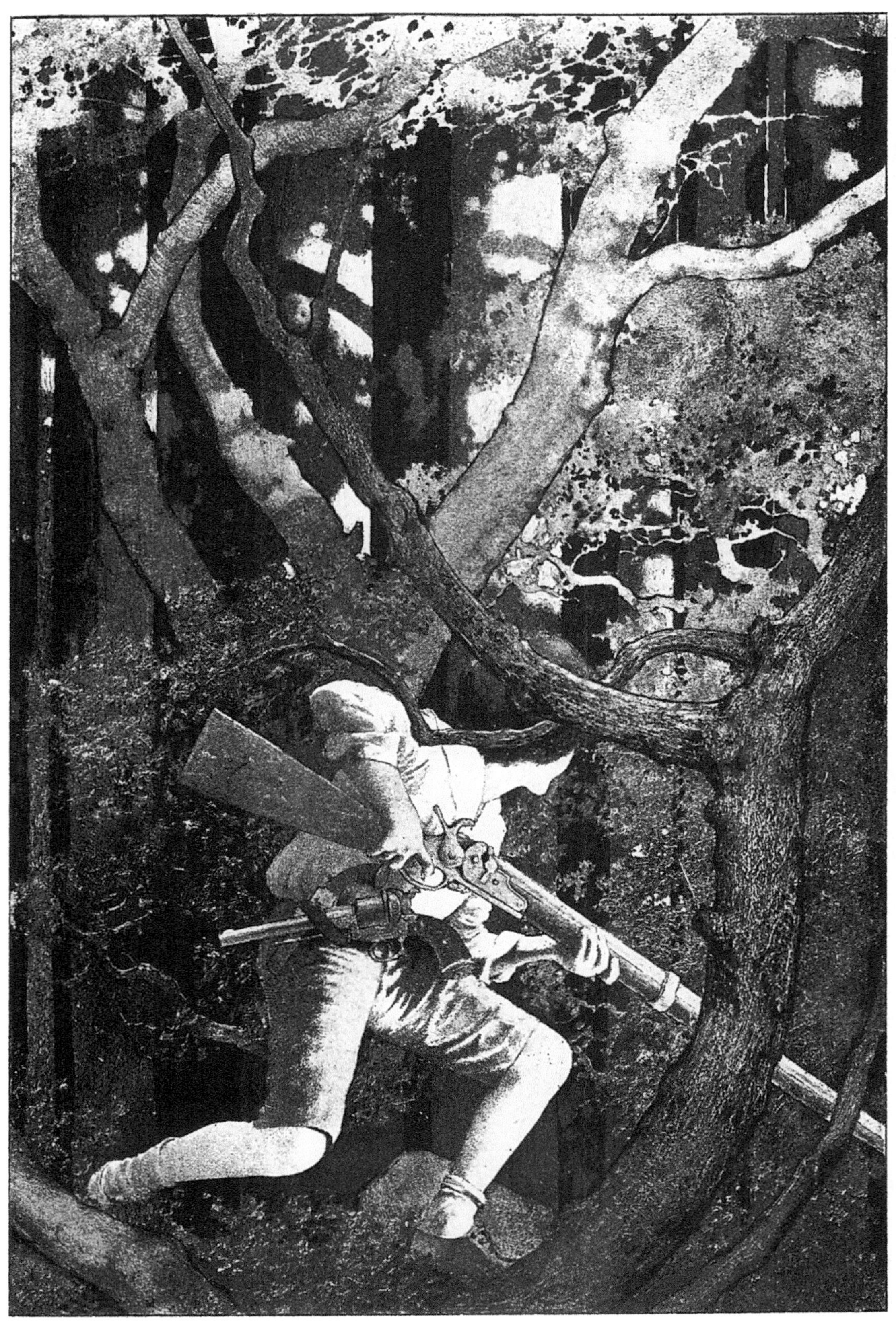

Plate 6.

It was easy . . . to transport yourself in a trice to the heart of a tropical forest
"Sawdust and Sin," *The Golden Age*, 1900

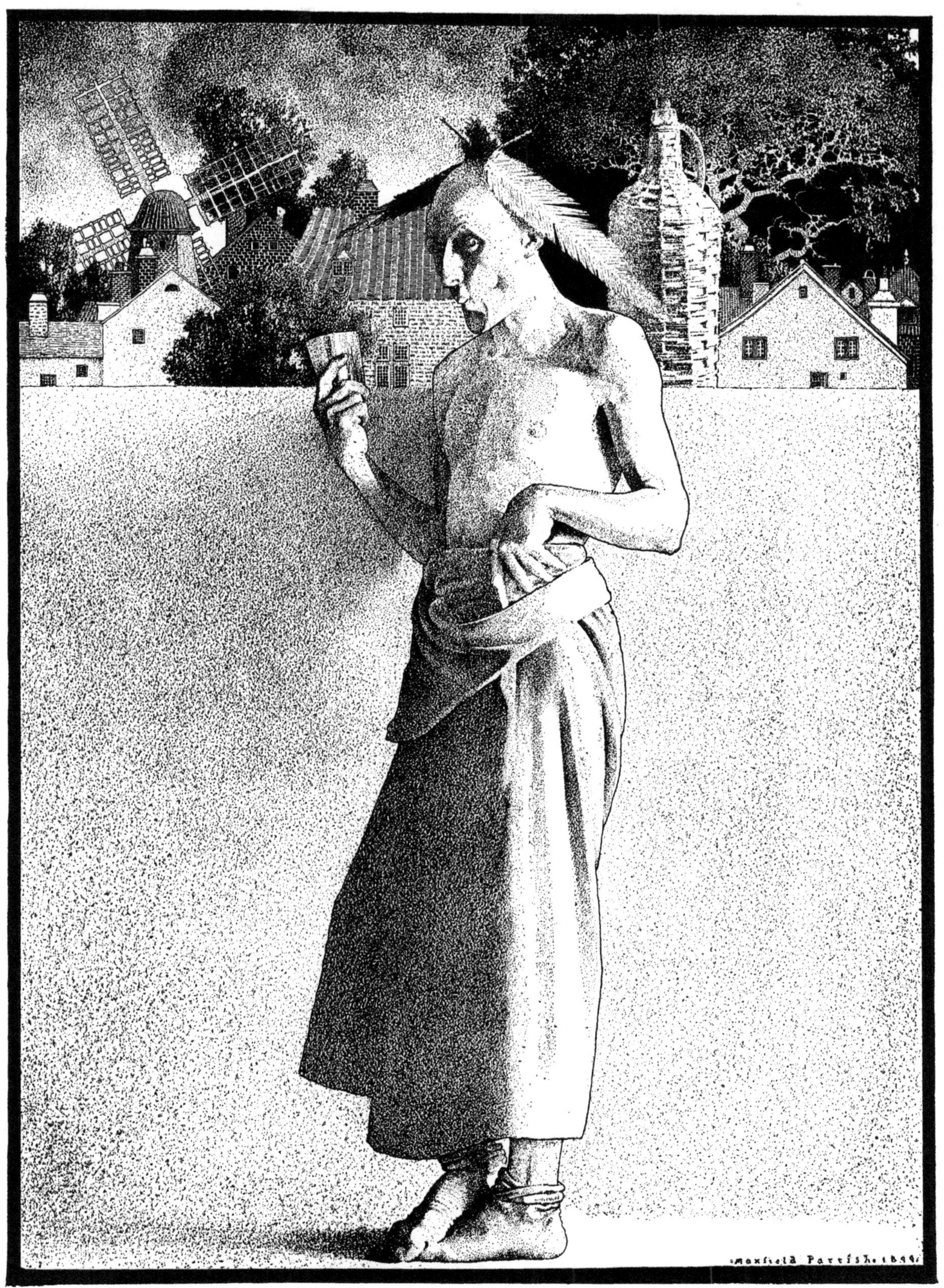

PLATE 7.

They introduced among them rum, gin, and brandy, and the other comforts of life
Knickerbocker's History of New York, 1900

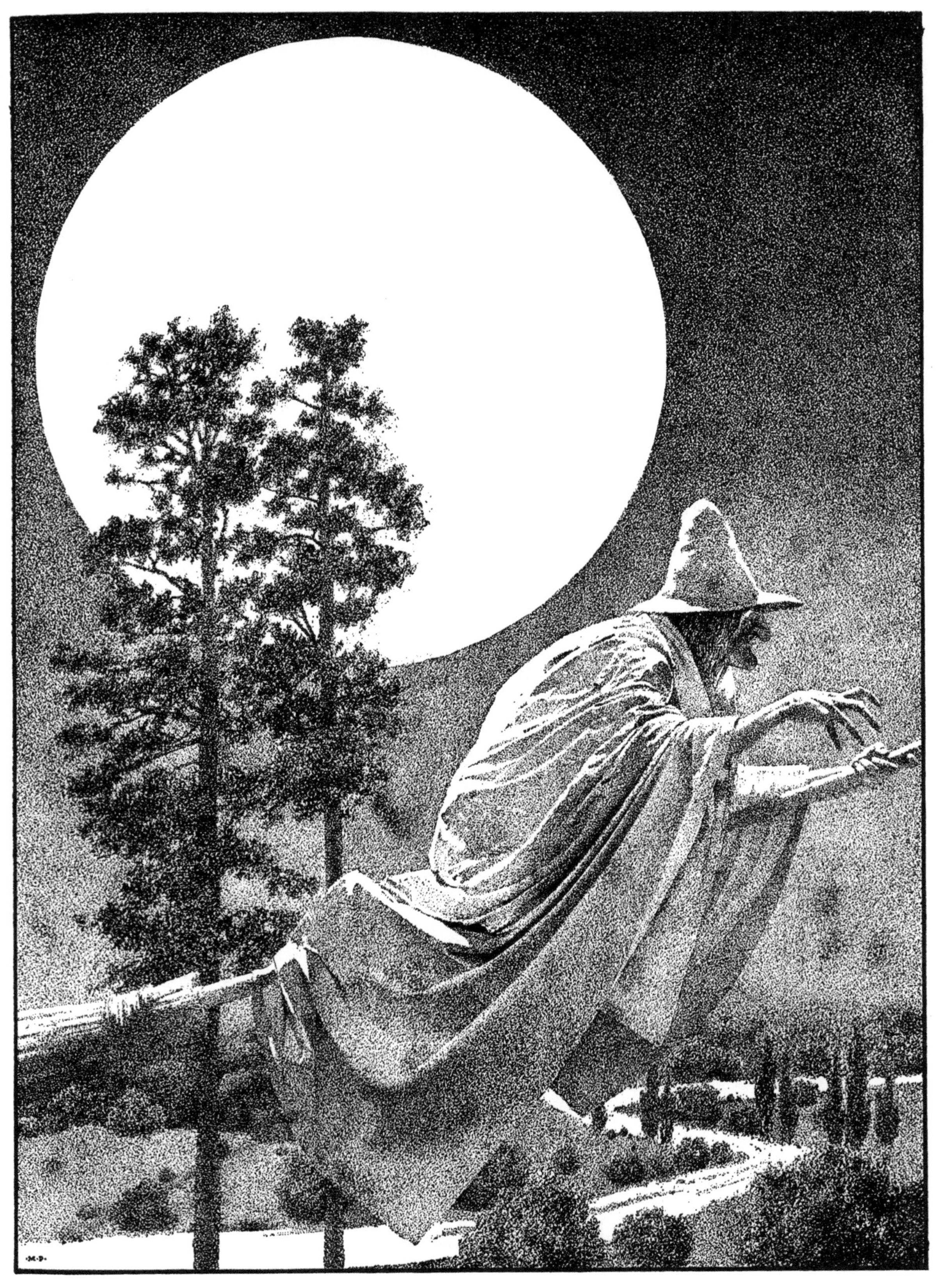

Plate 8.

Concerning witchcraft superstitions
Knickerbocker's History of New York, 1900

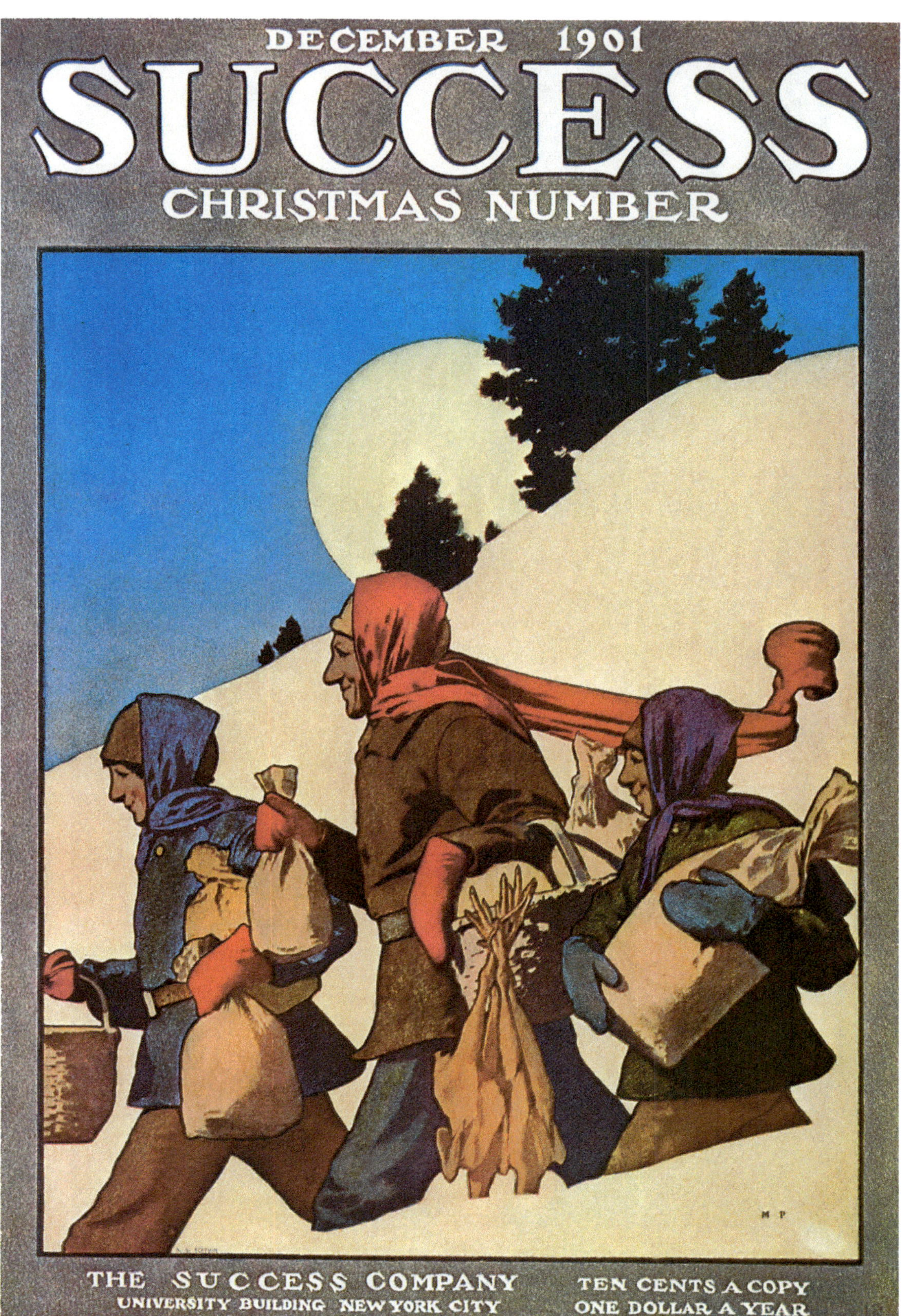

Plate 9.

Cover
Success magazine, December 1901

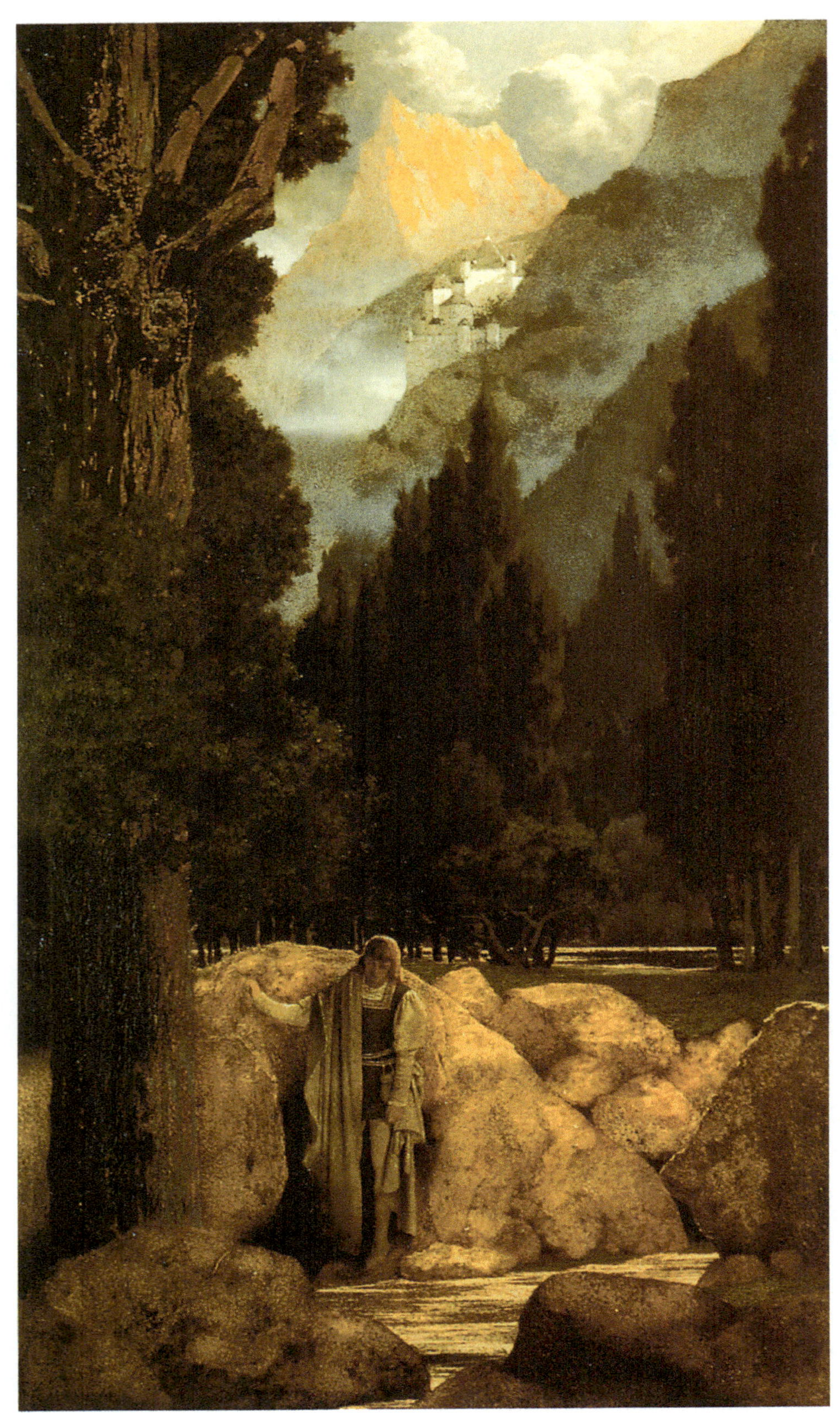

Plate 10.

Poet's Dream
(for John Milton's "L'Allegro")
Century Magazine, December 1901

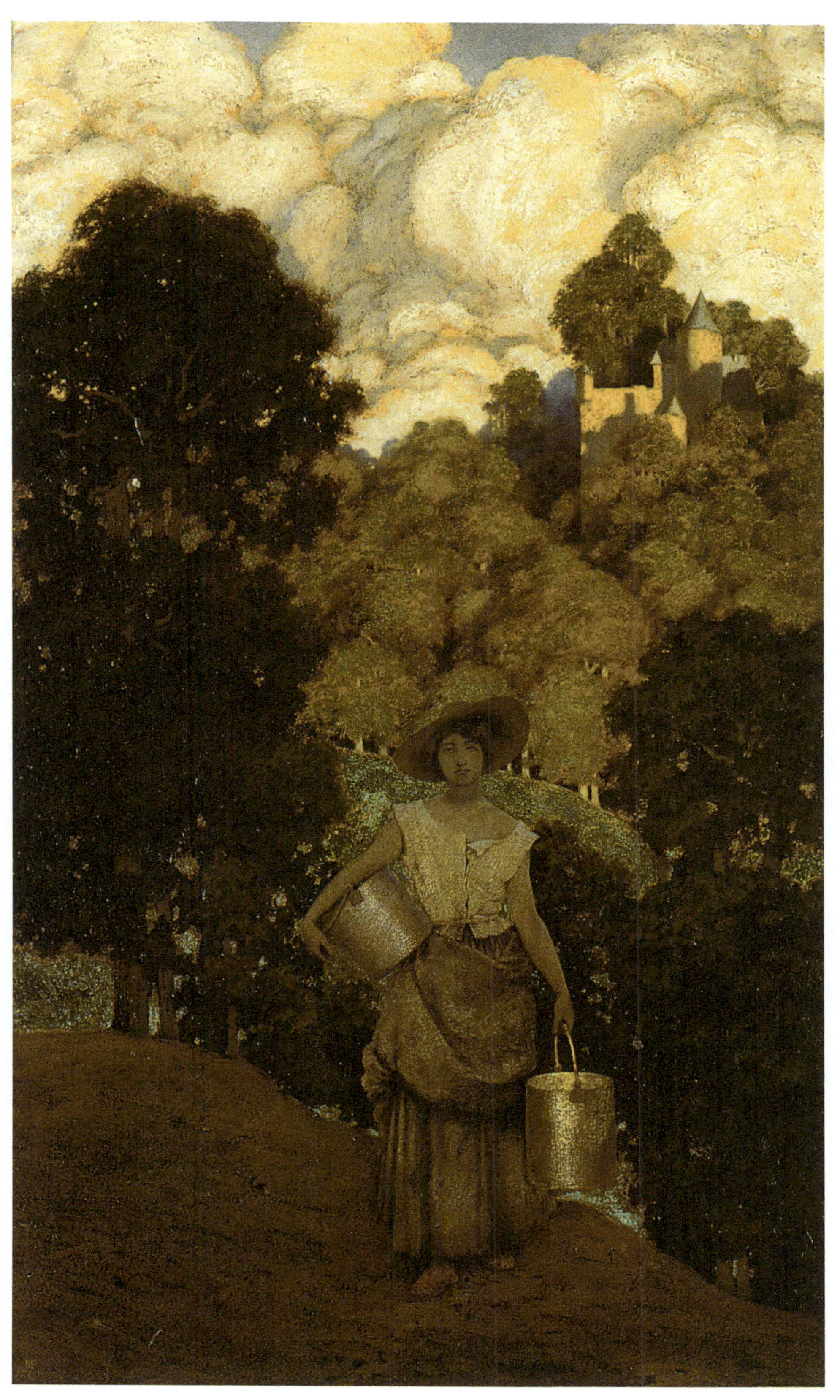

Plate 11.

The Milkmaid
(for John Milton's "L'Allegro")
Century Magazine, December 1901

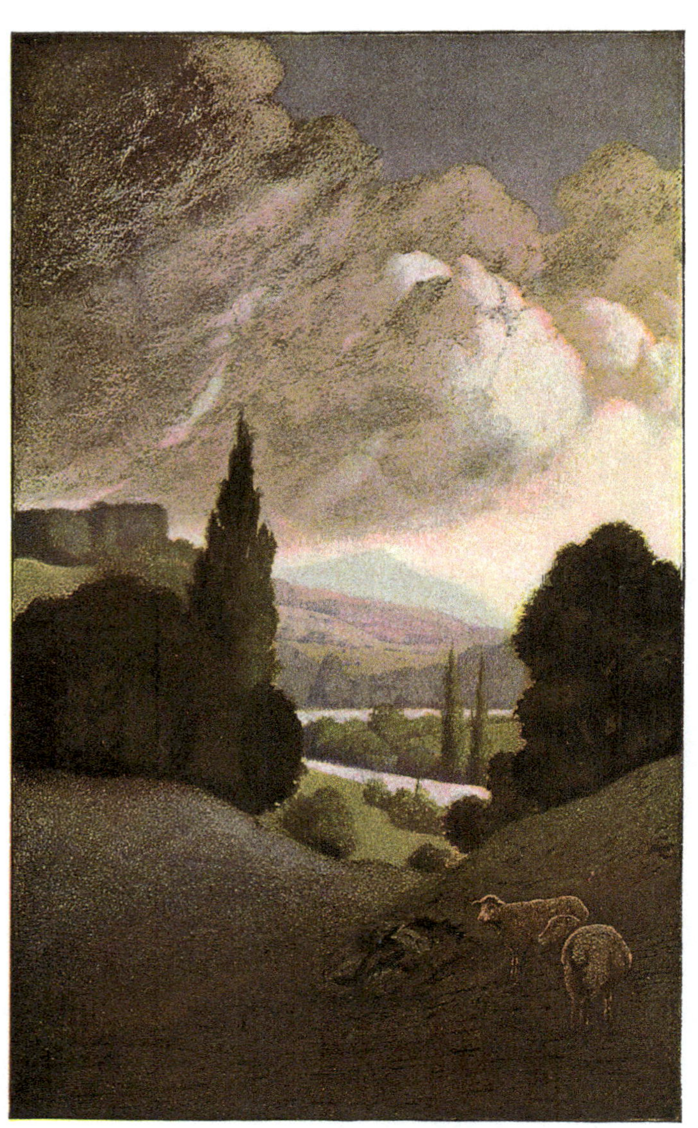

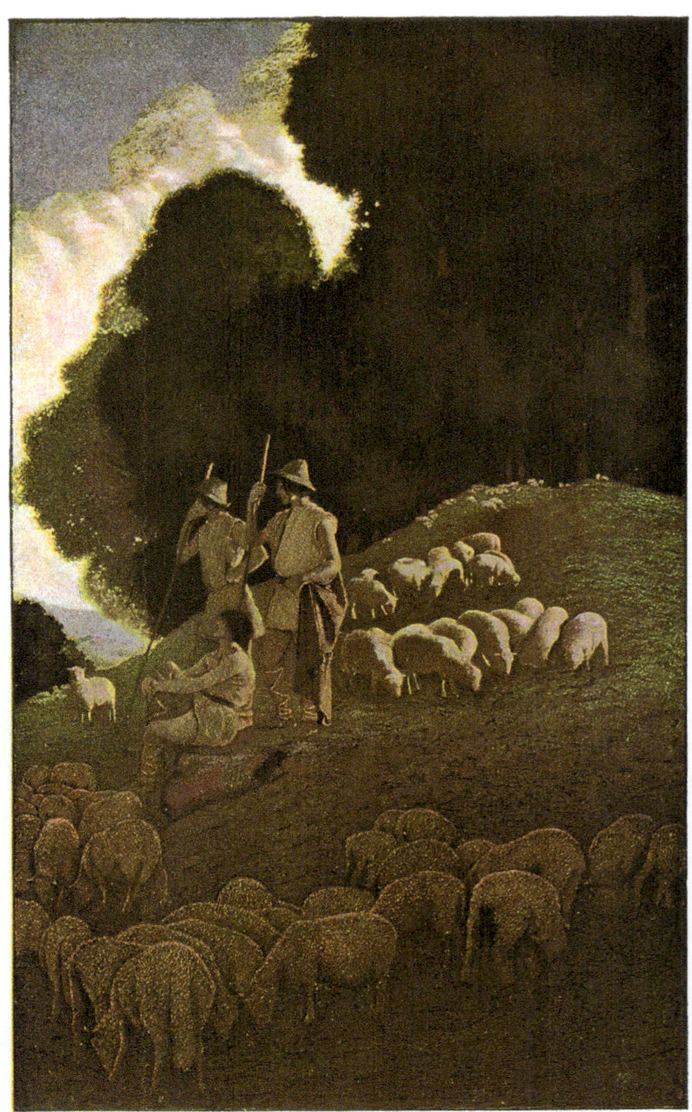

Plate 12.

"Straight mine eye hath caught new pleasures" (diptych)
(for John Milton's "L'Allegro")
Century Magazine, December 1901

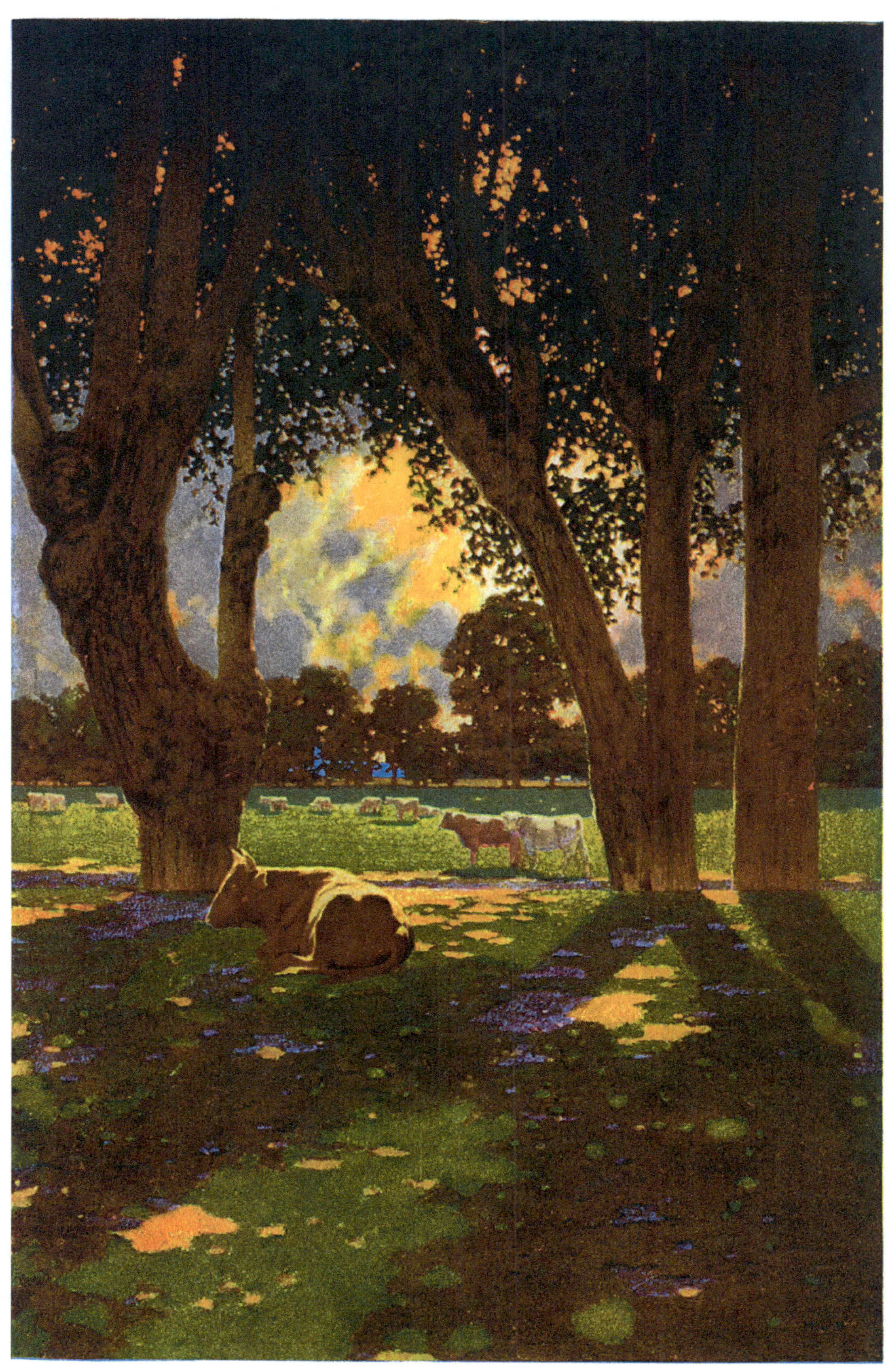

Plate 13.

The Desert with Water (Cows)
"The Great Southwest"
Century Magazine, 1902

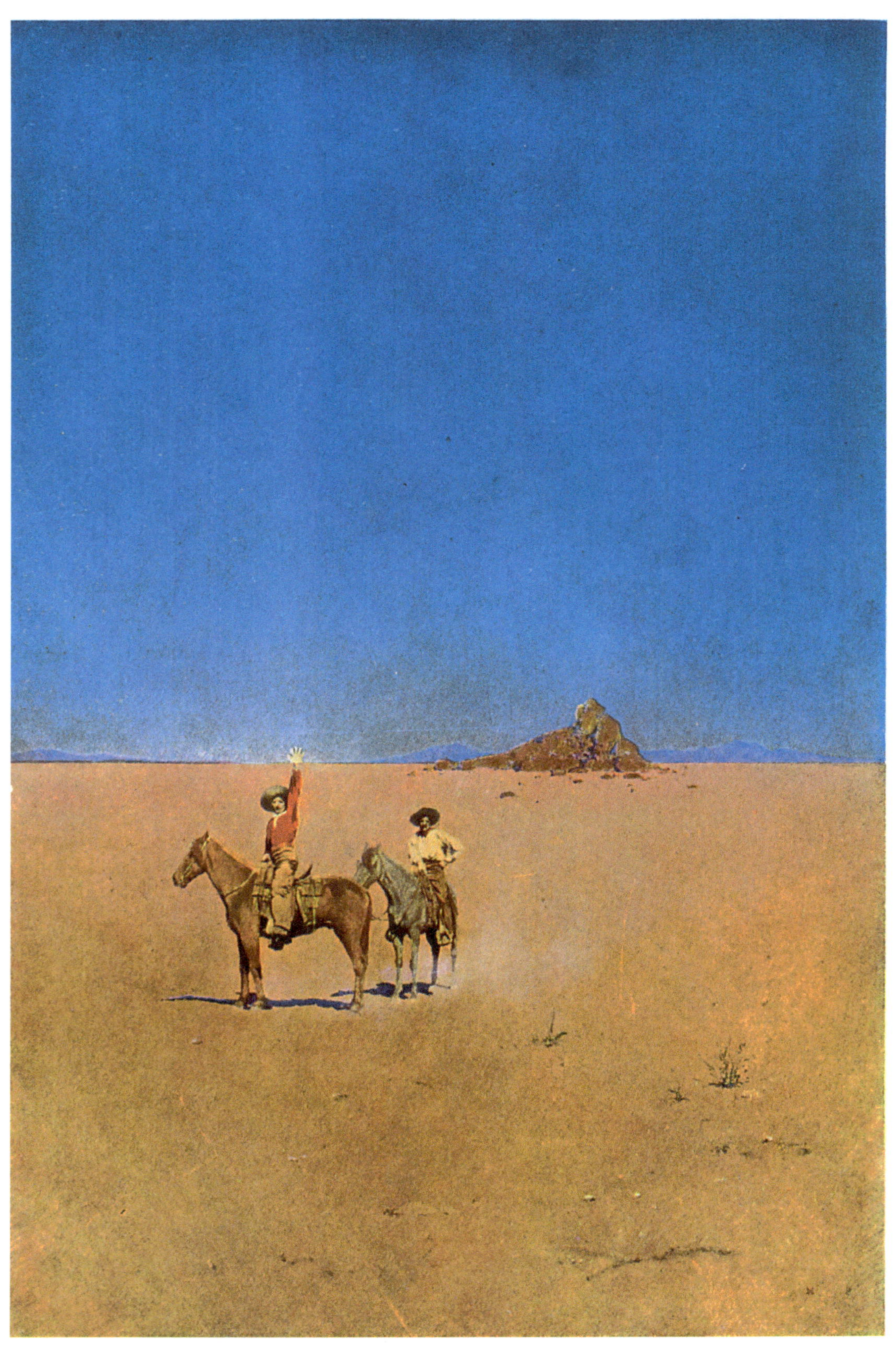

Plate 14.

The Desert without Water (Cowboys)
"The Great Southwest"
Century Magazine, 1902

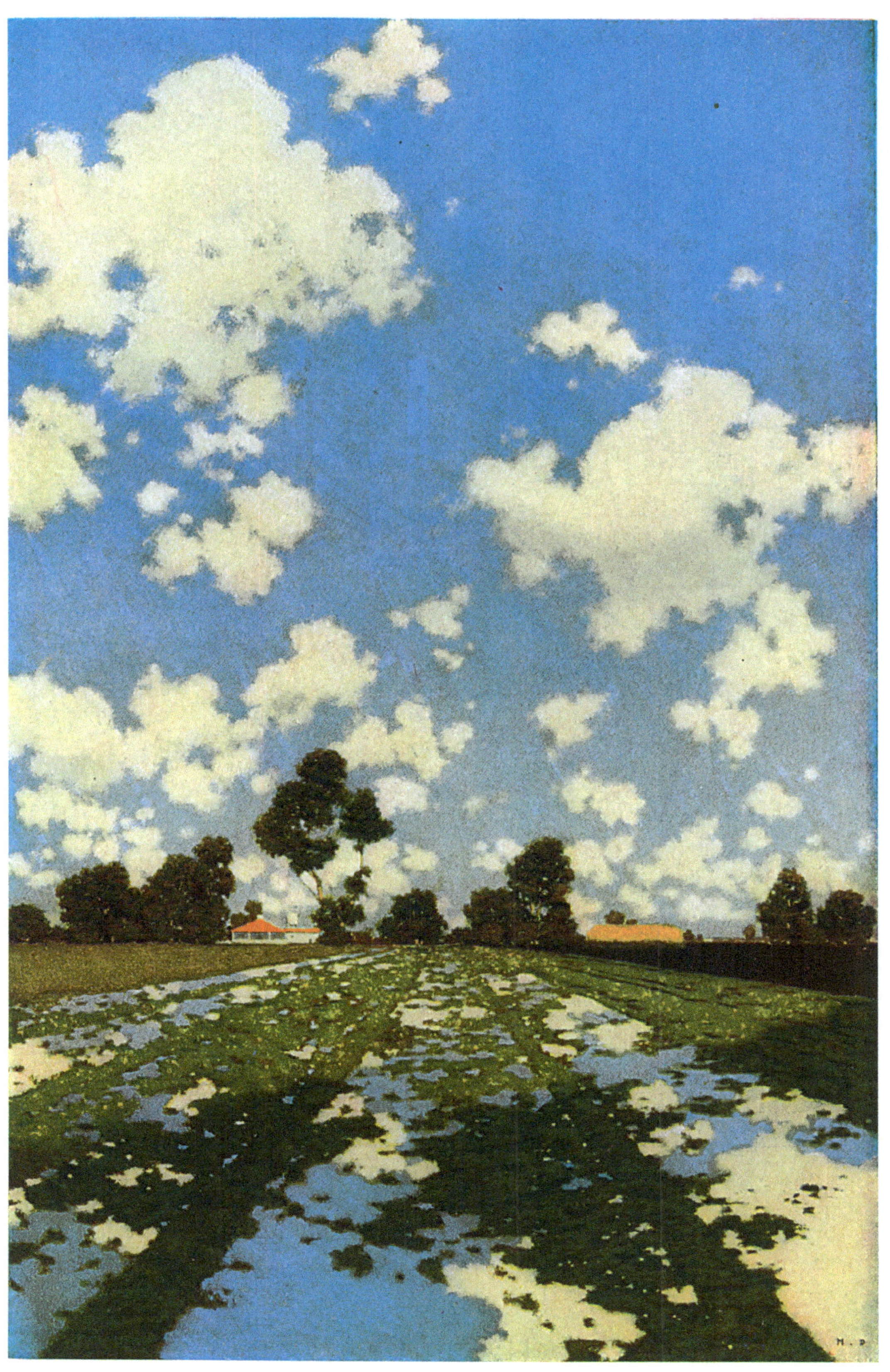

Plate 15.

Water Let in on a Field of Alfalfa
"The Great Southwest"
Century Magazine, 1902

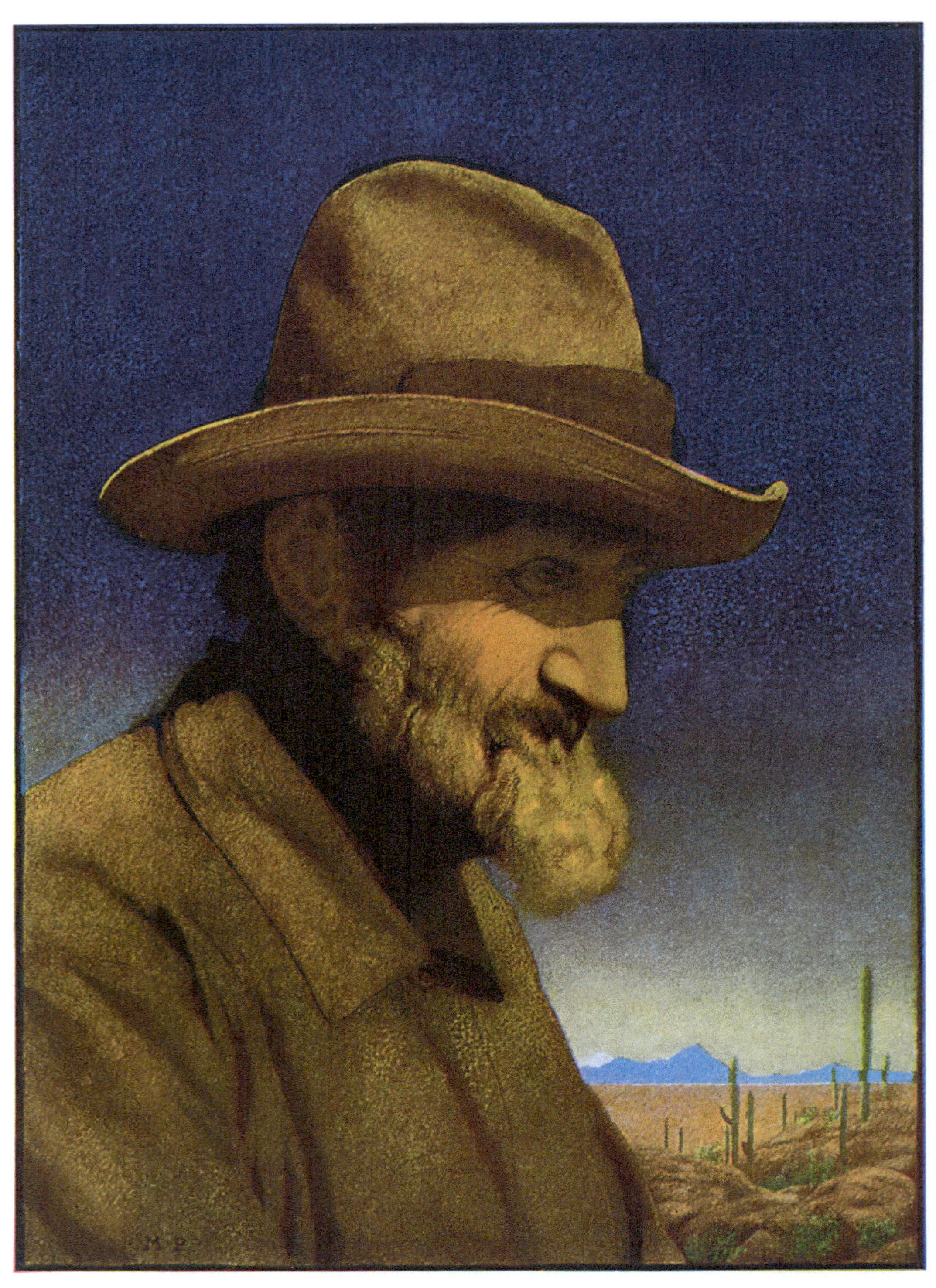

Plate 16.

Bill Sachs
"The Great Southwest"
Century Magazine, 1902

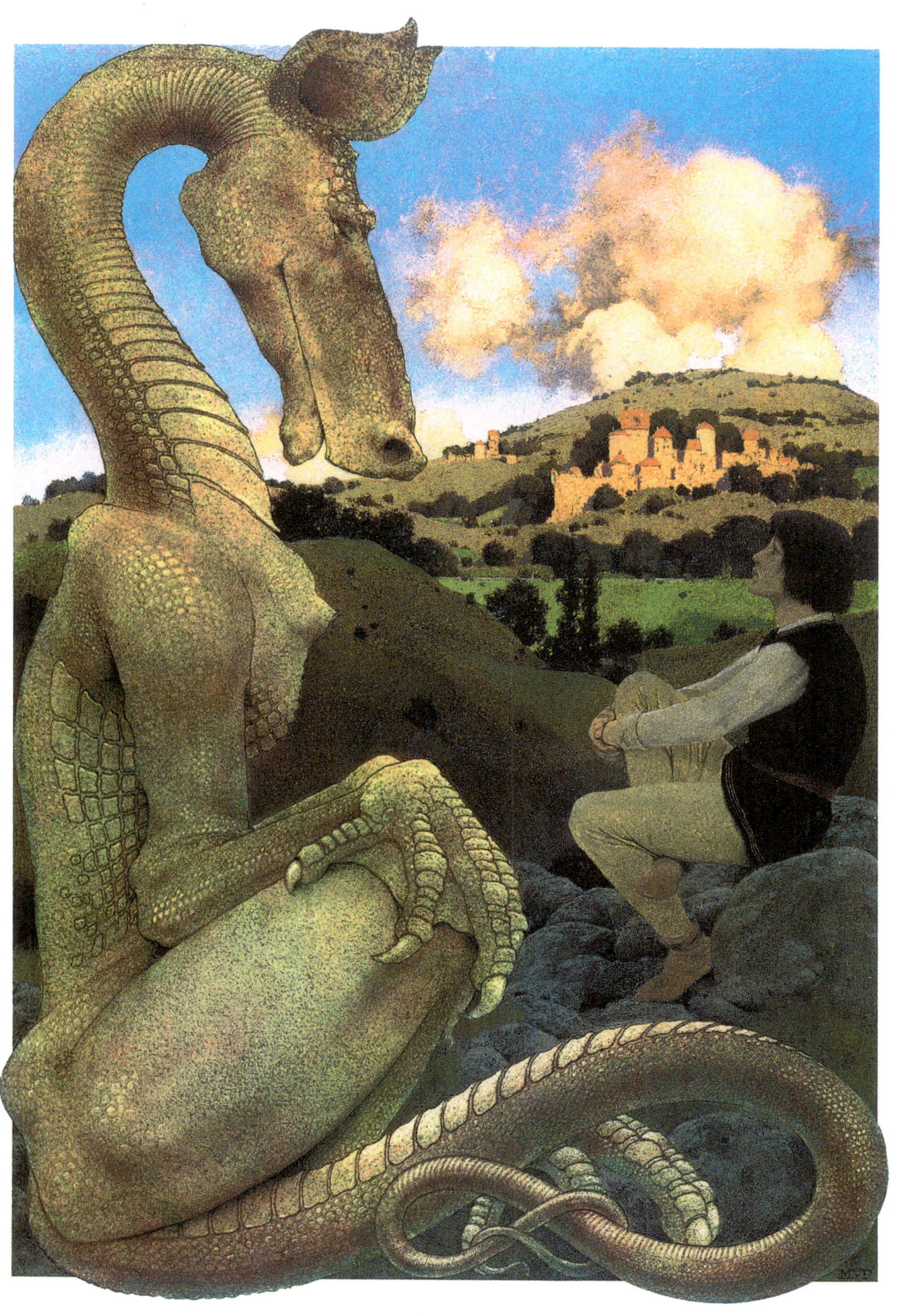

Plate 17.

The Reluctant Dragon
Dream Days, 1902

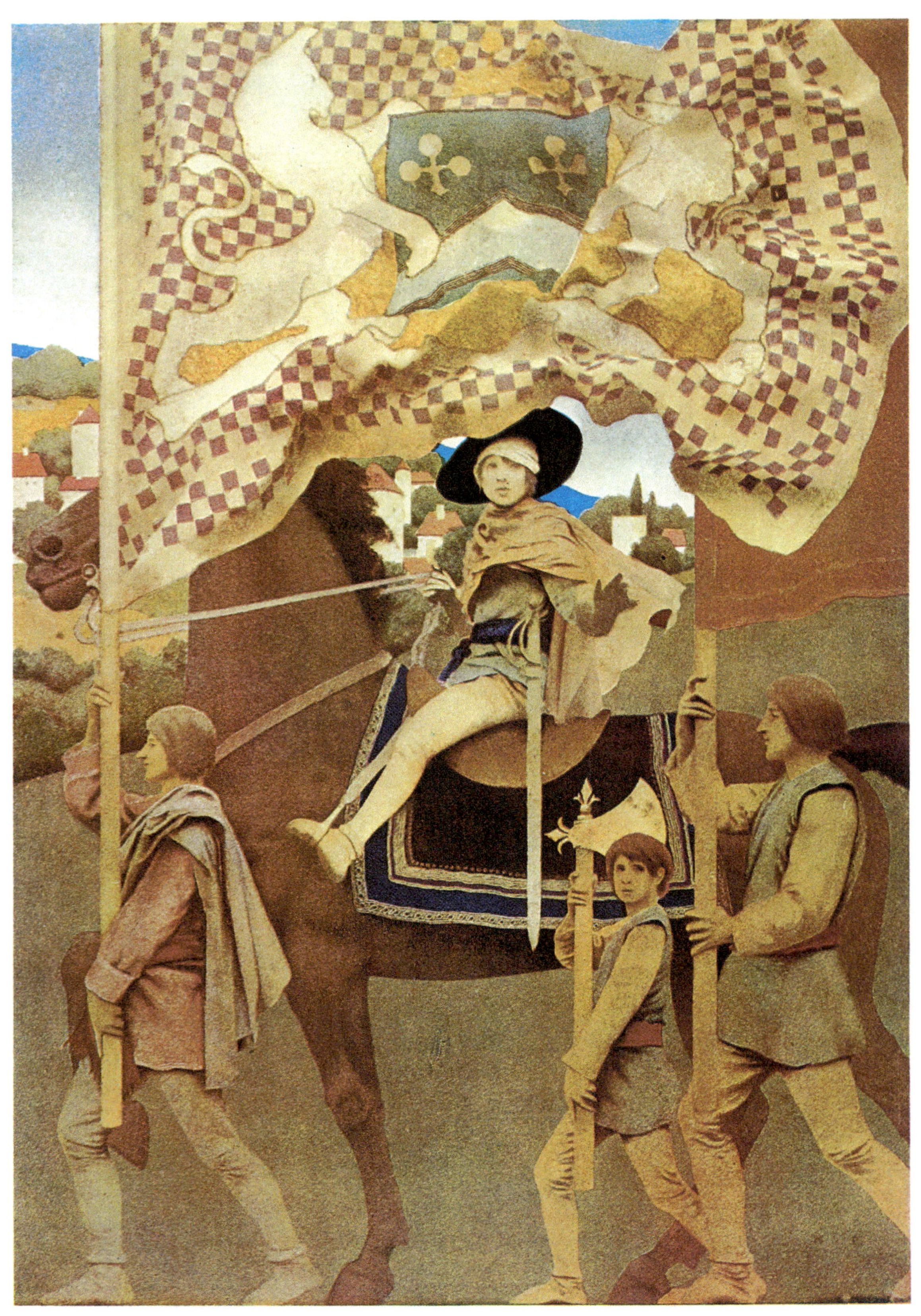

Plate 18.

Dies Irae
Dream Days, 1902

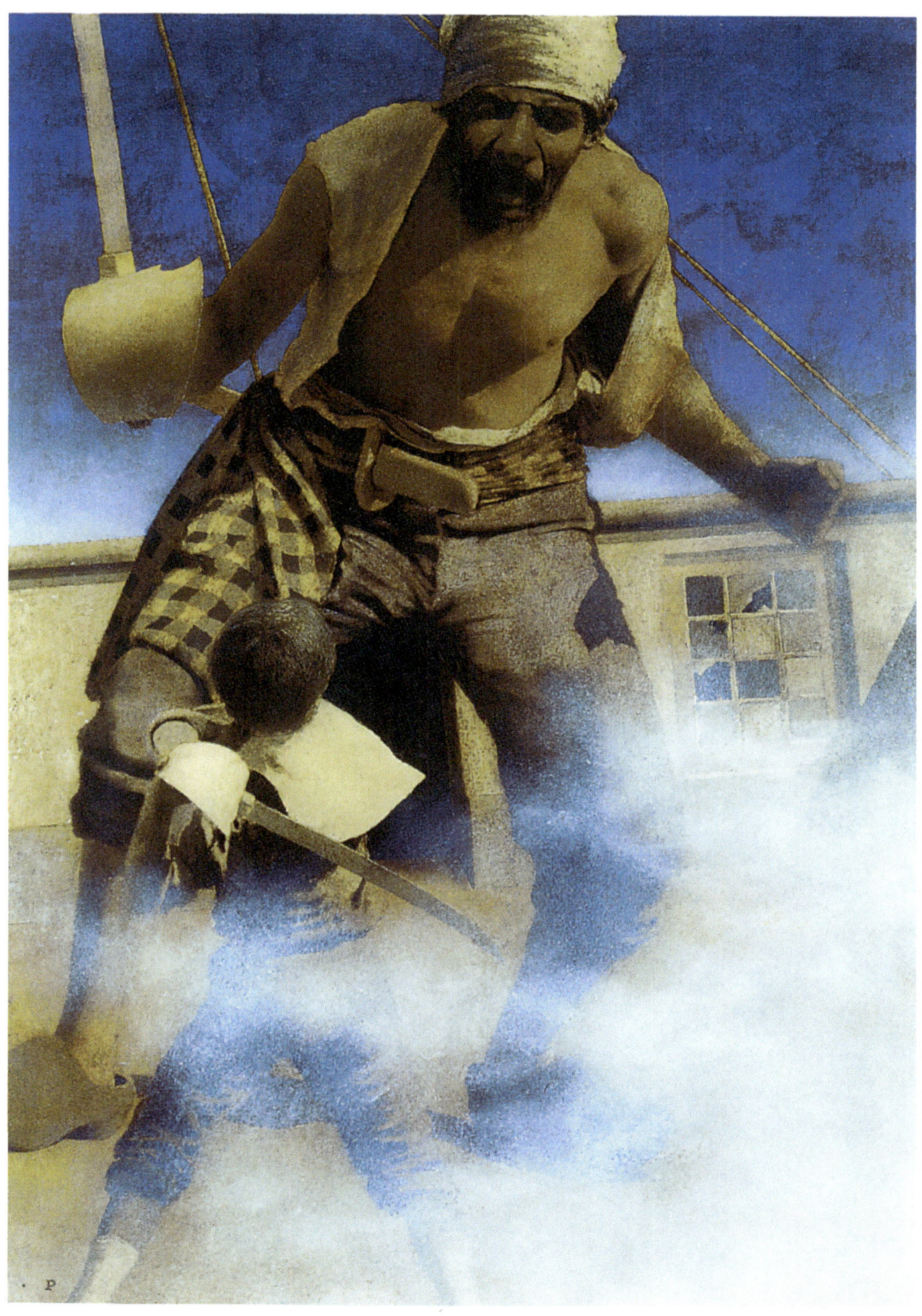

Plate 19.

A Saga of the Seas
Dream Days, 1902

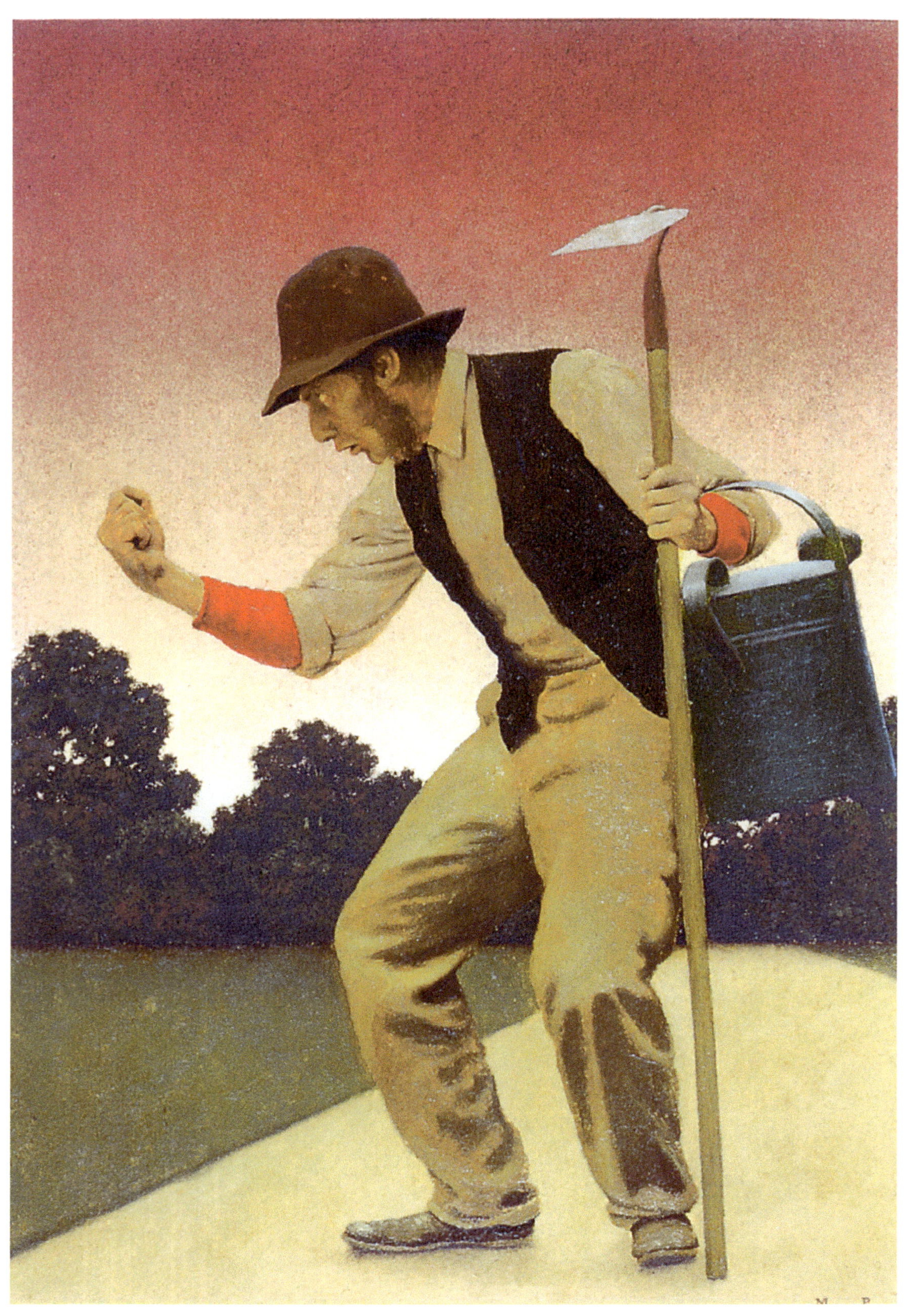

Plate 20.

The Twenty-first of October
Dream Days, 1902

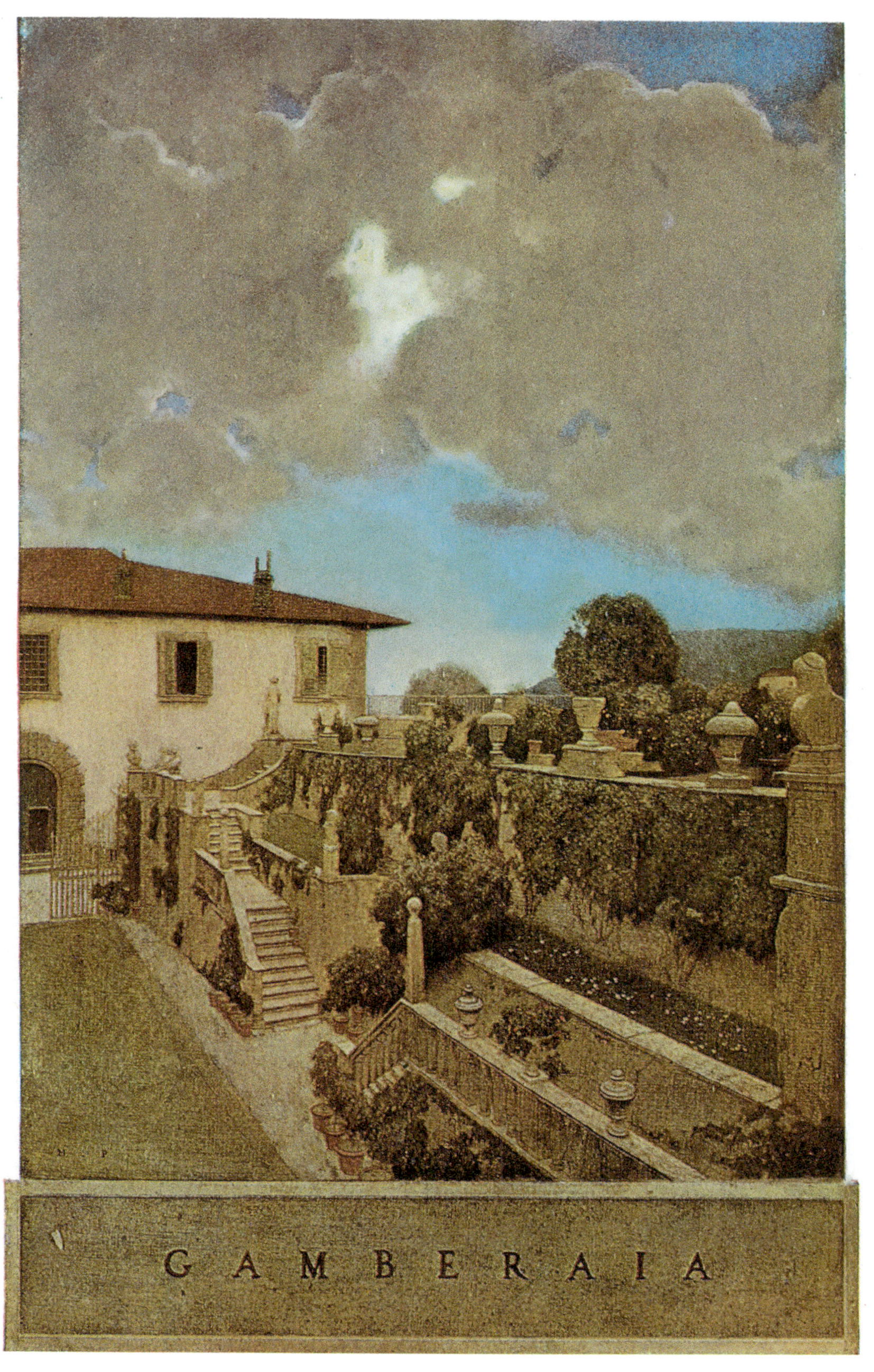

Plate 21.

Villa Gamberaia, near Florence

Century Magazine, November 1904

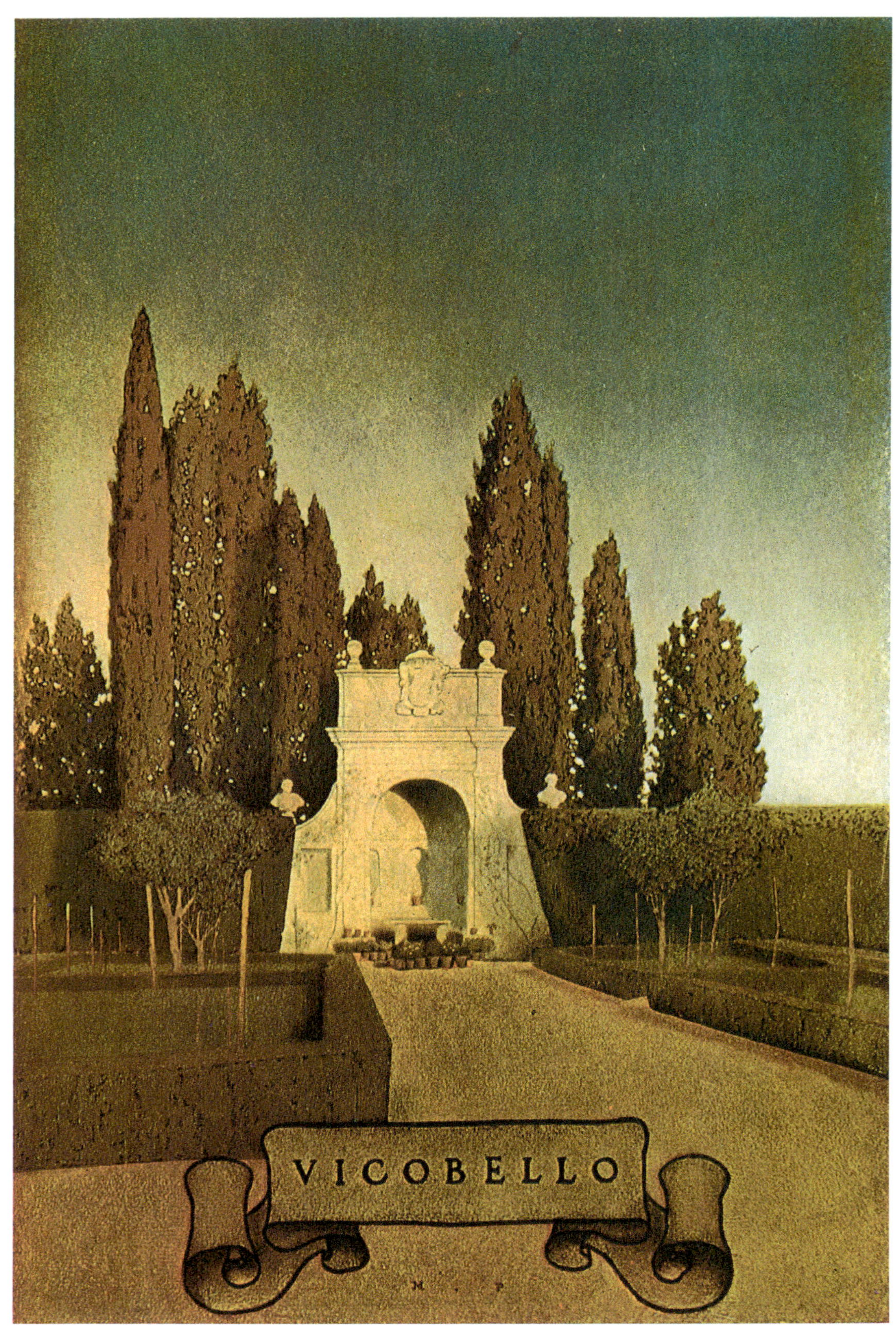

Plate 22.

Vicobello, Siena
"Italian Villas and Their Gardens"
Century Magazine, November 1904

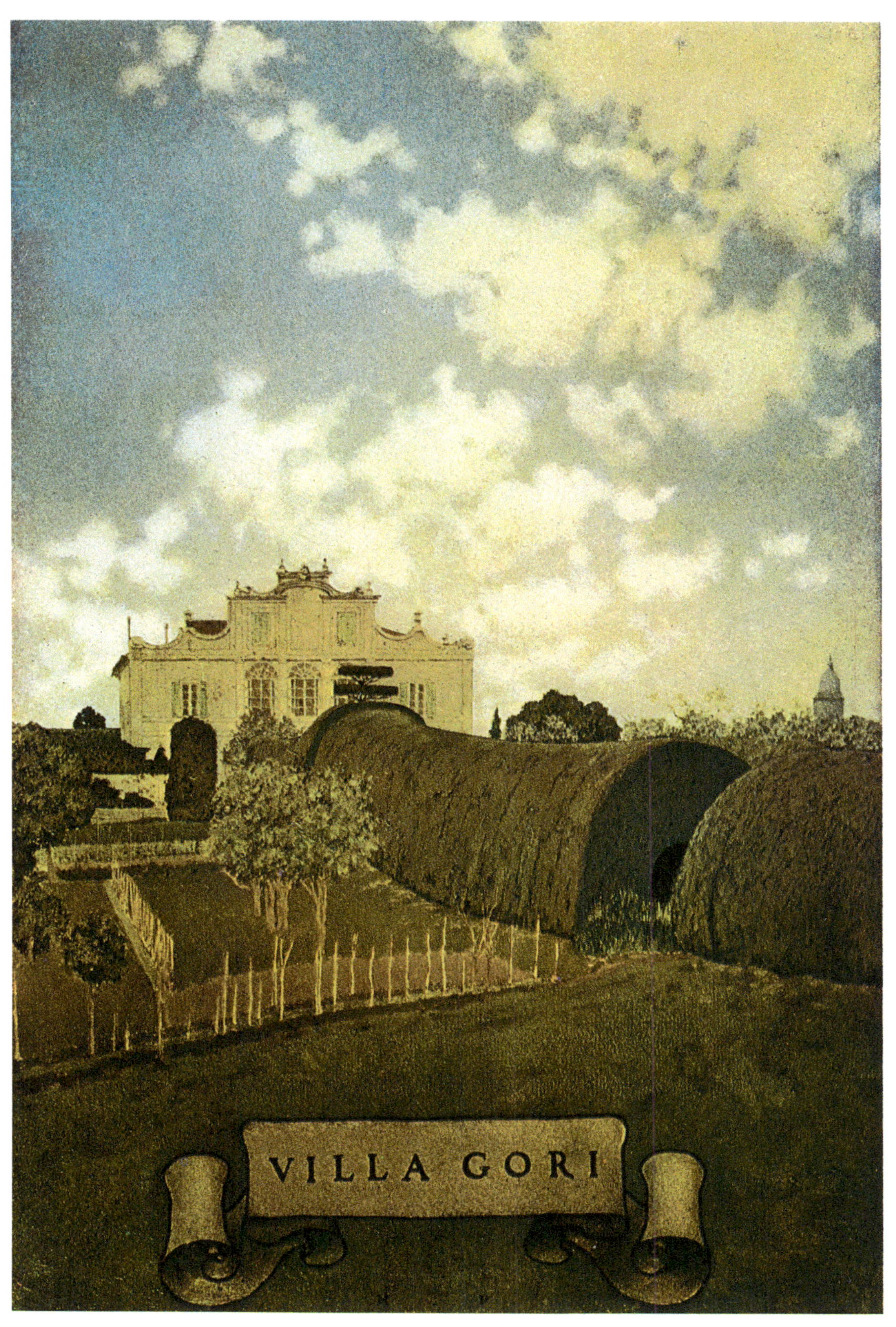

Plate 23.

La Palazzina [Villa Gori], Siena
"Italian Villas and Their Gardens"
Century Magazine, November 1904

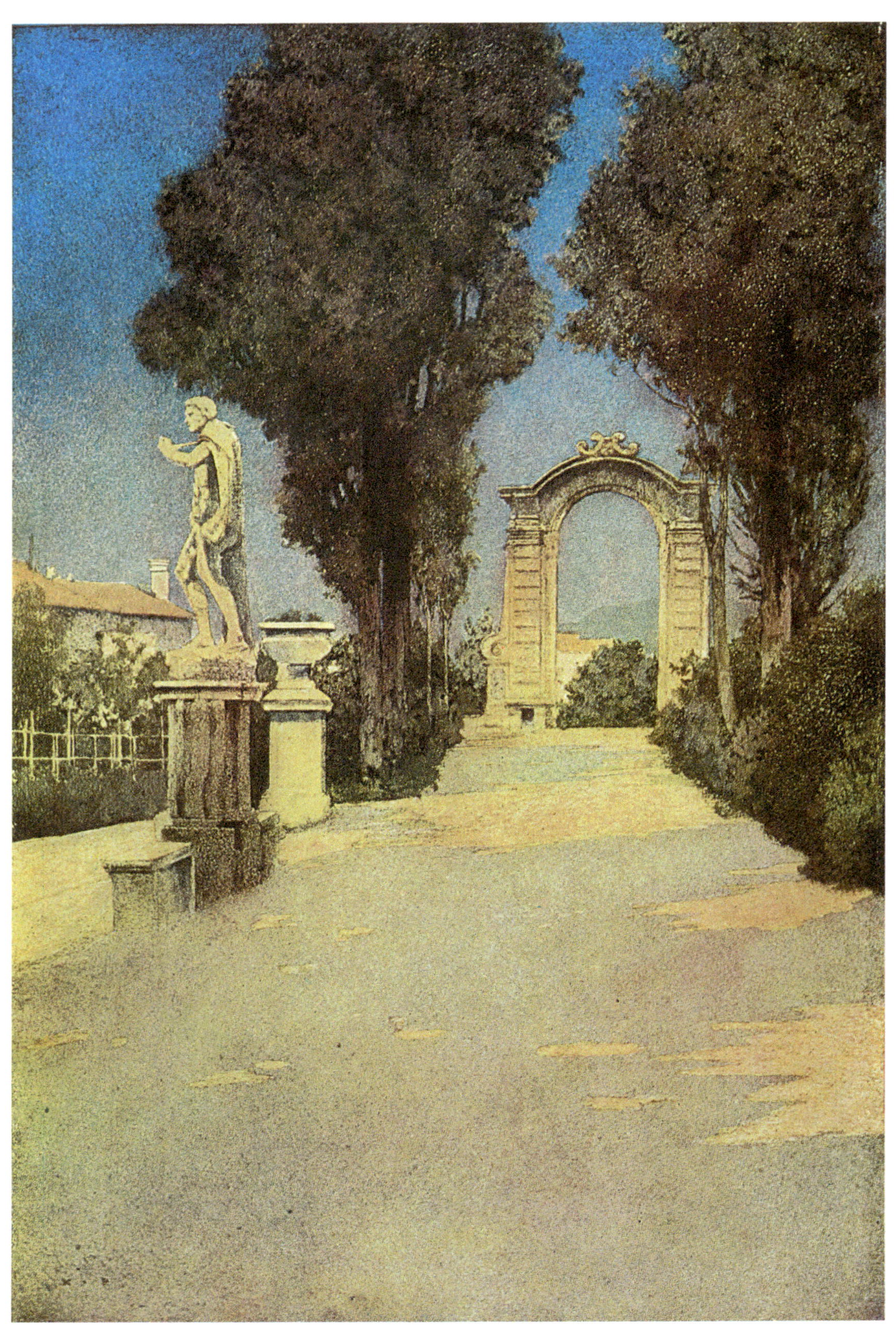

Plate 24.

Villa Scassi, Genoa
"Italian Villas and Their Gardens"
Century Magazine, November 1904

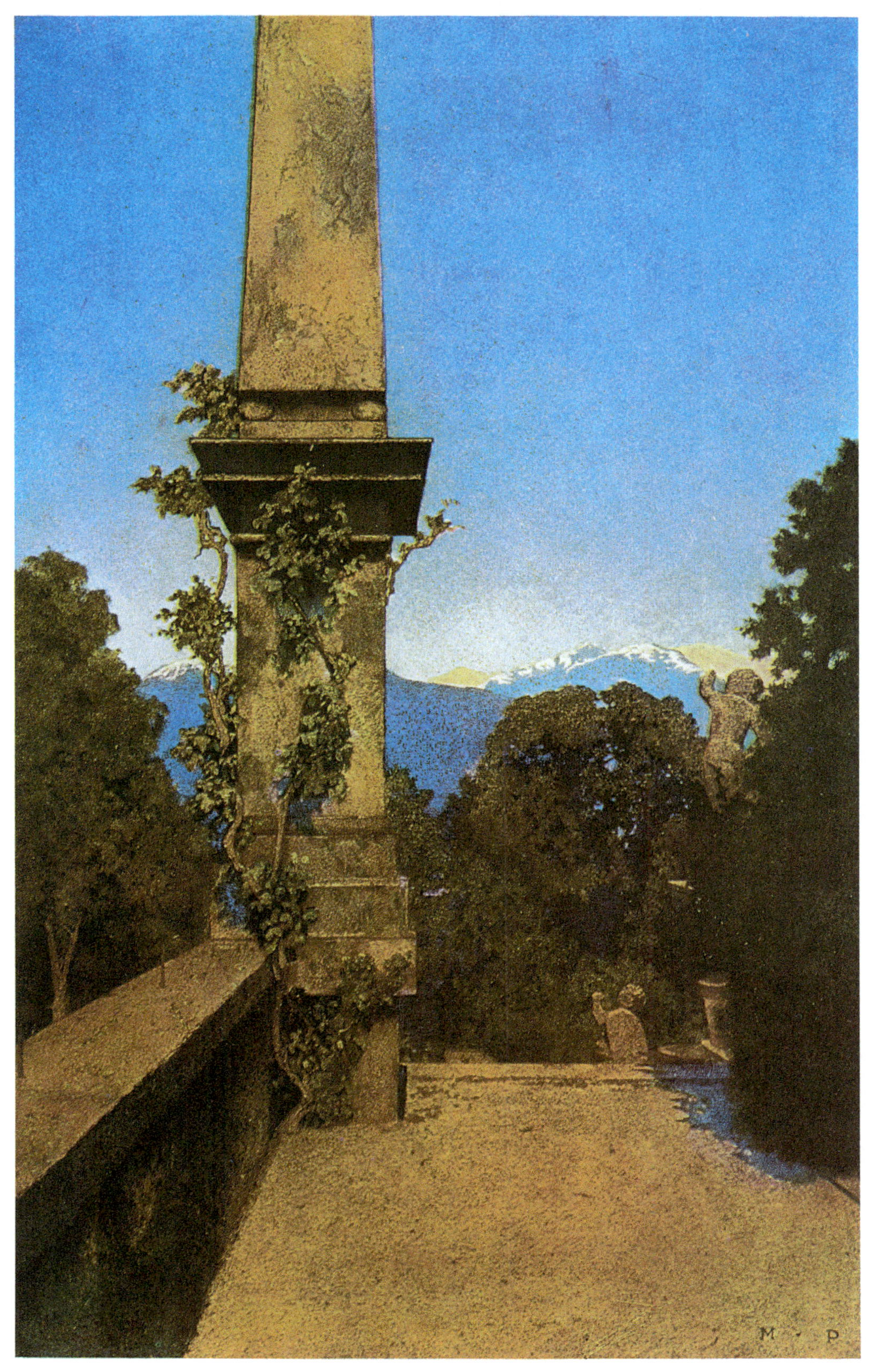

Plate 25.

In the Gardens of Isola Bella, Lake Maggiore
"Italian Villas and Their Gardens"
Century Magazine, November 1904

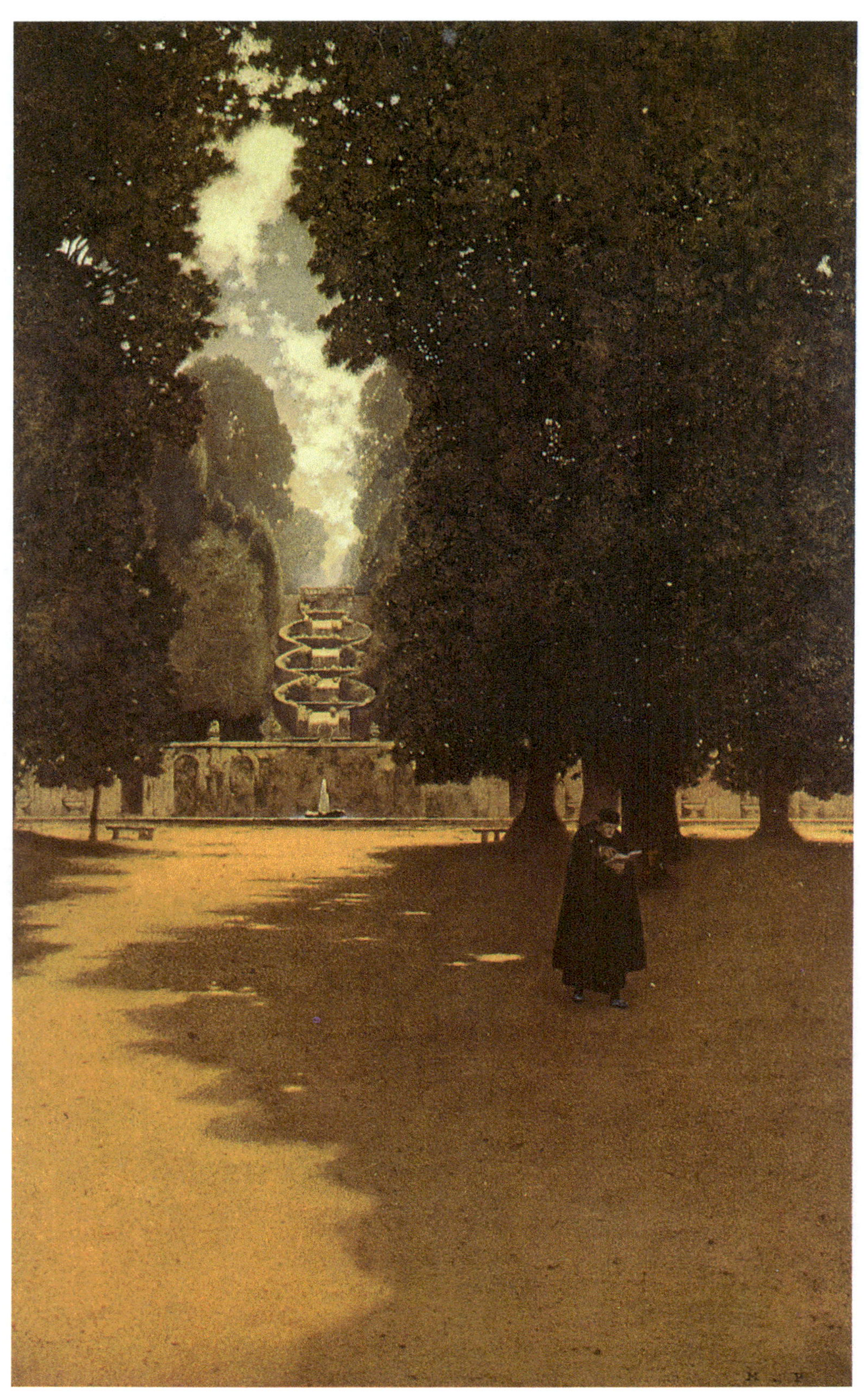

Plate 26.

Villa Torlonia, Rome
"Italian Villas and Their Gardens"
Century Magazine, November 1904

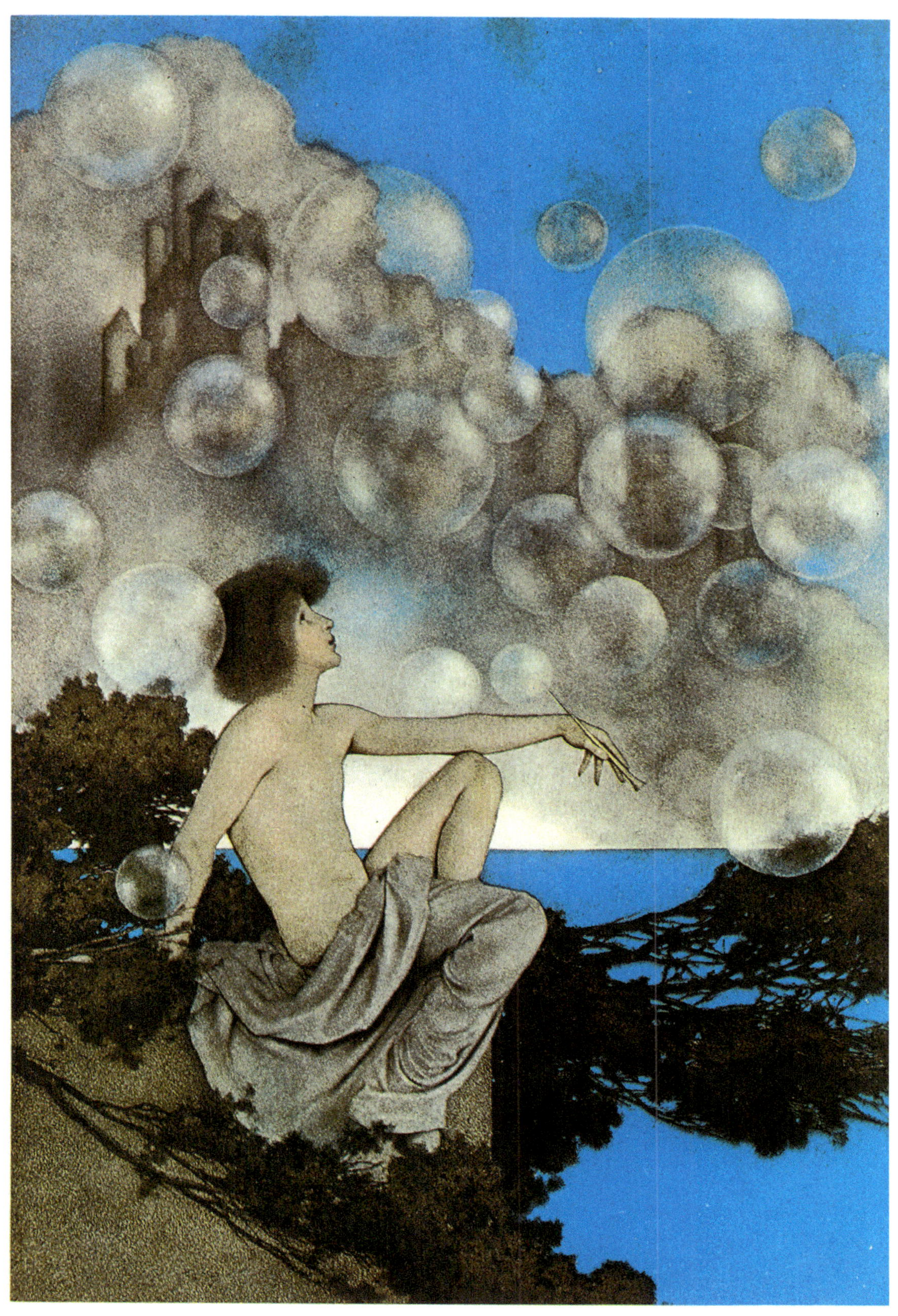

Plate 27.

Air Castles
Cover, *Ladies' Home Journal*, 1904

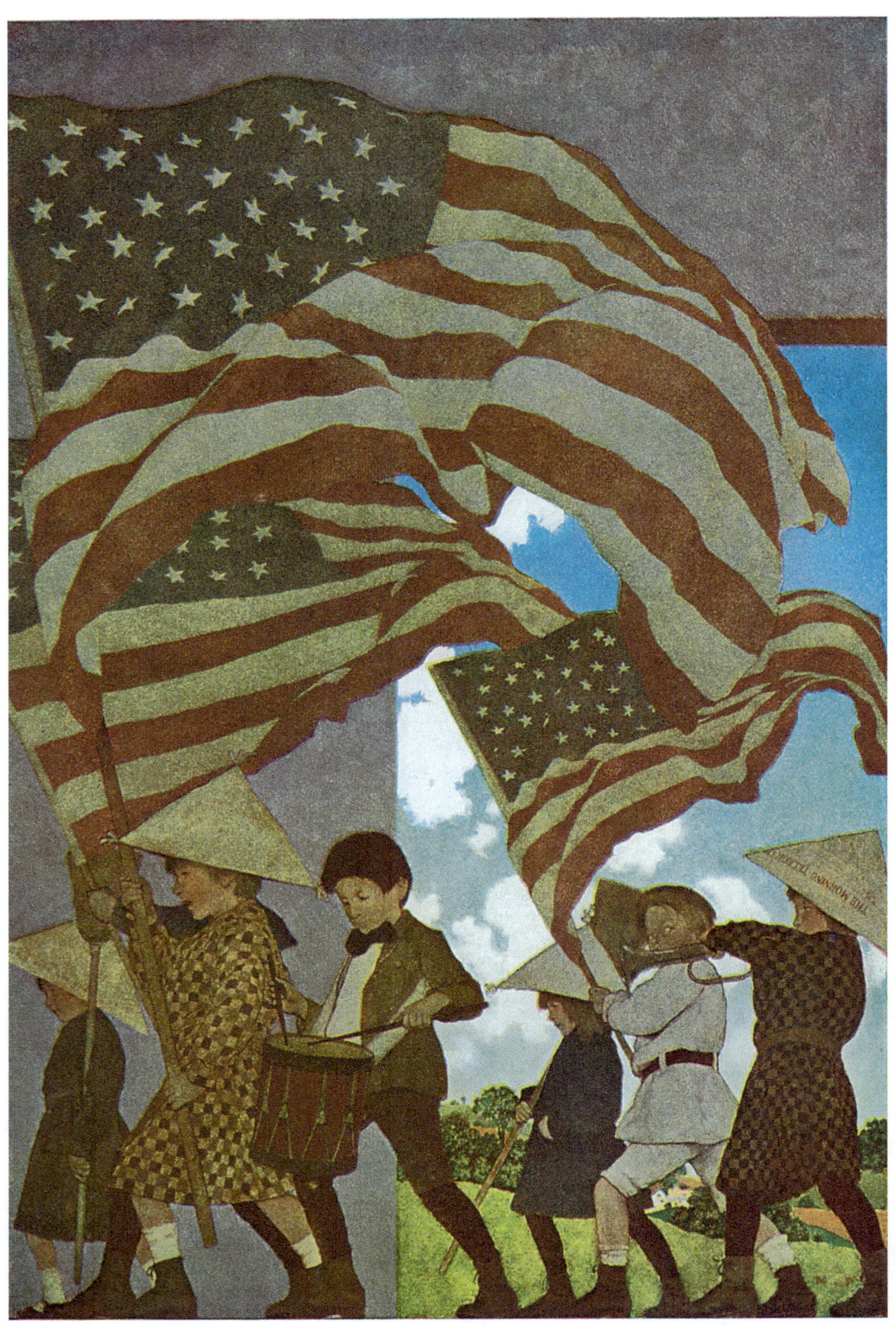

Plate 28.

"With Trumpet and Drum"

With big tin trumpet and little red drum,
Marching like soldiers, the children come!

Poems of Childhood, 1904

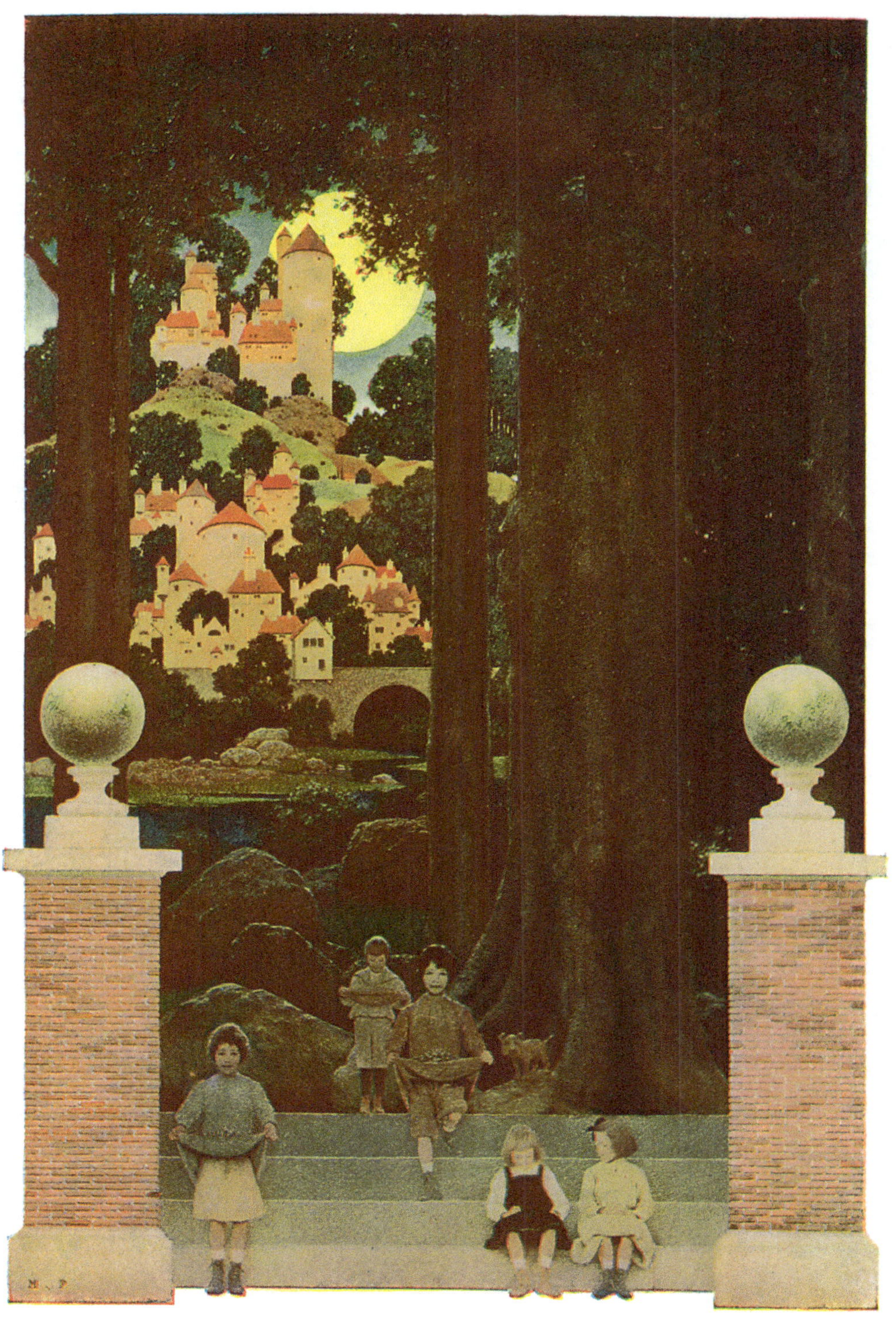

Plate 29.

"The Sugar-Plum Tree"

And you carry away of the treasure that rains
As much as your apron can hold!

Poems of Childhood, 1904

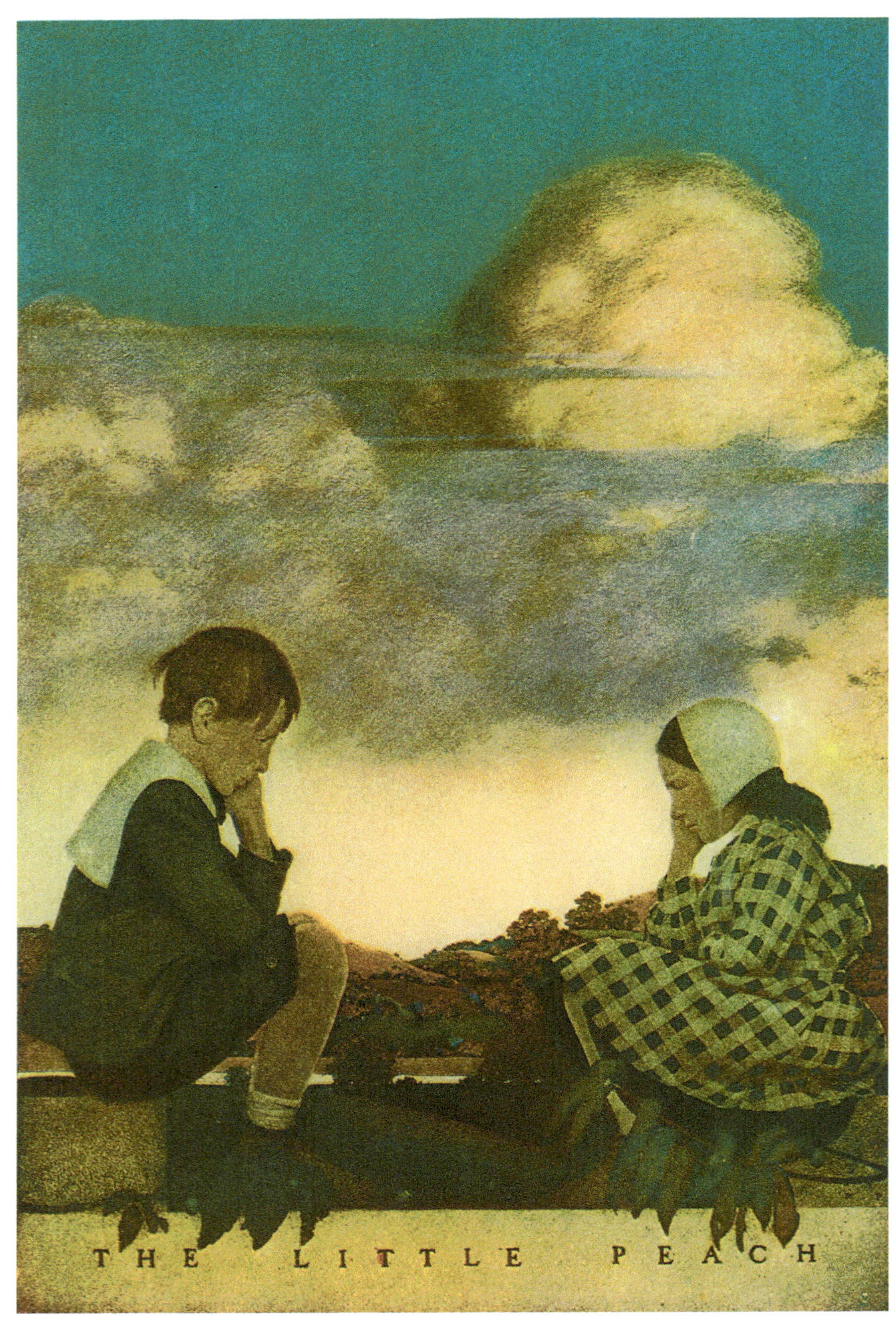

Plate 30.

"The Little Peach"

John took a bite and Sue a chew,
And then the trouble began to brew,—
Trouble the doctor couldn't subdue.
Too true!

Poems of Childhood, 1904

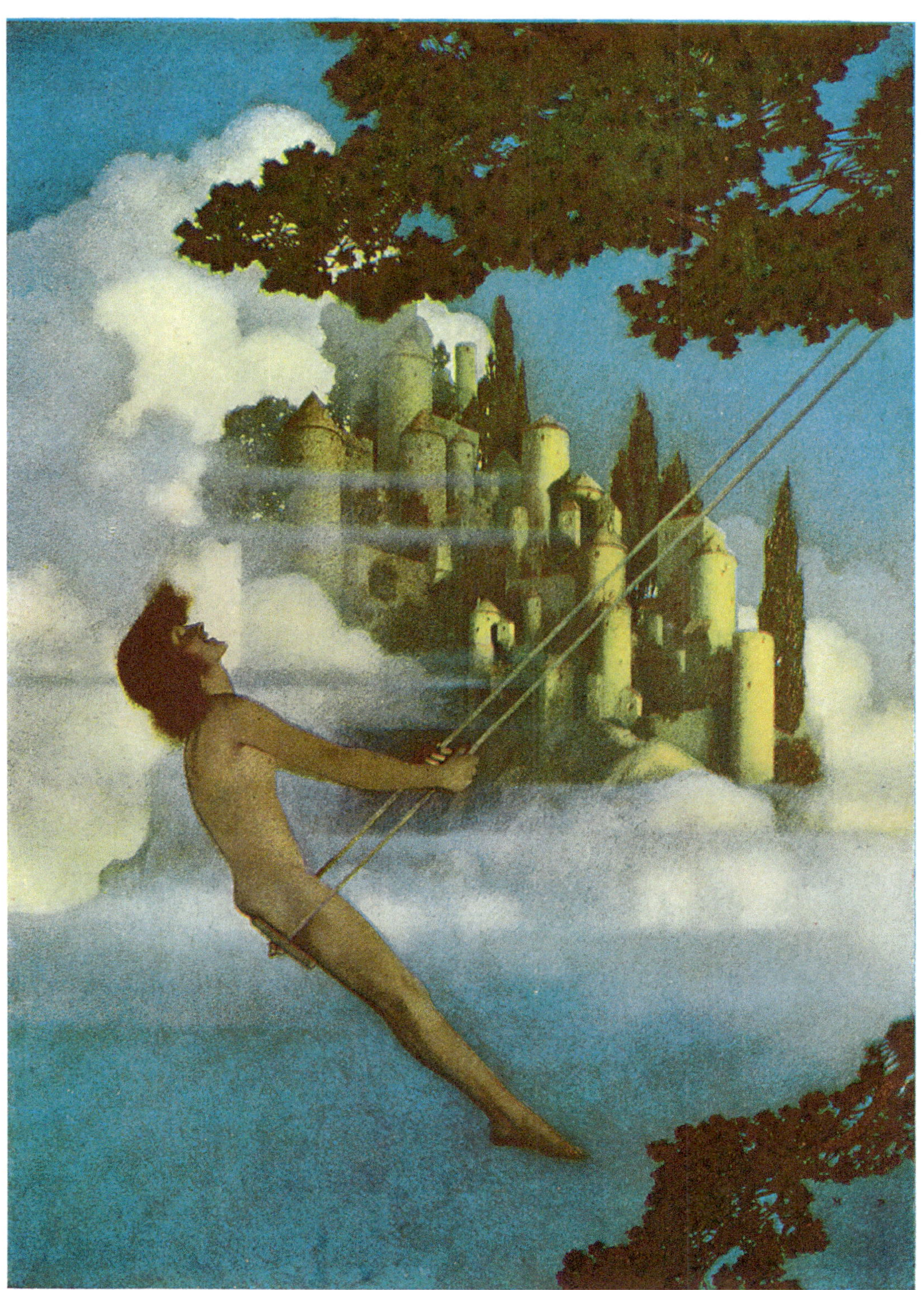

Plate 31.

"The Dinkey-Bird"

In an ocean, 'way out yonder
(As all sapient people know),
Is the land of Wonder-Wander,
Whither children love to go.

Poems of Childhood, 1904

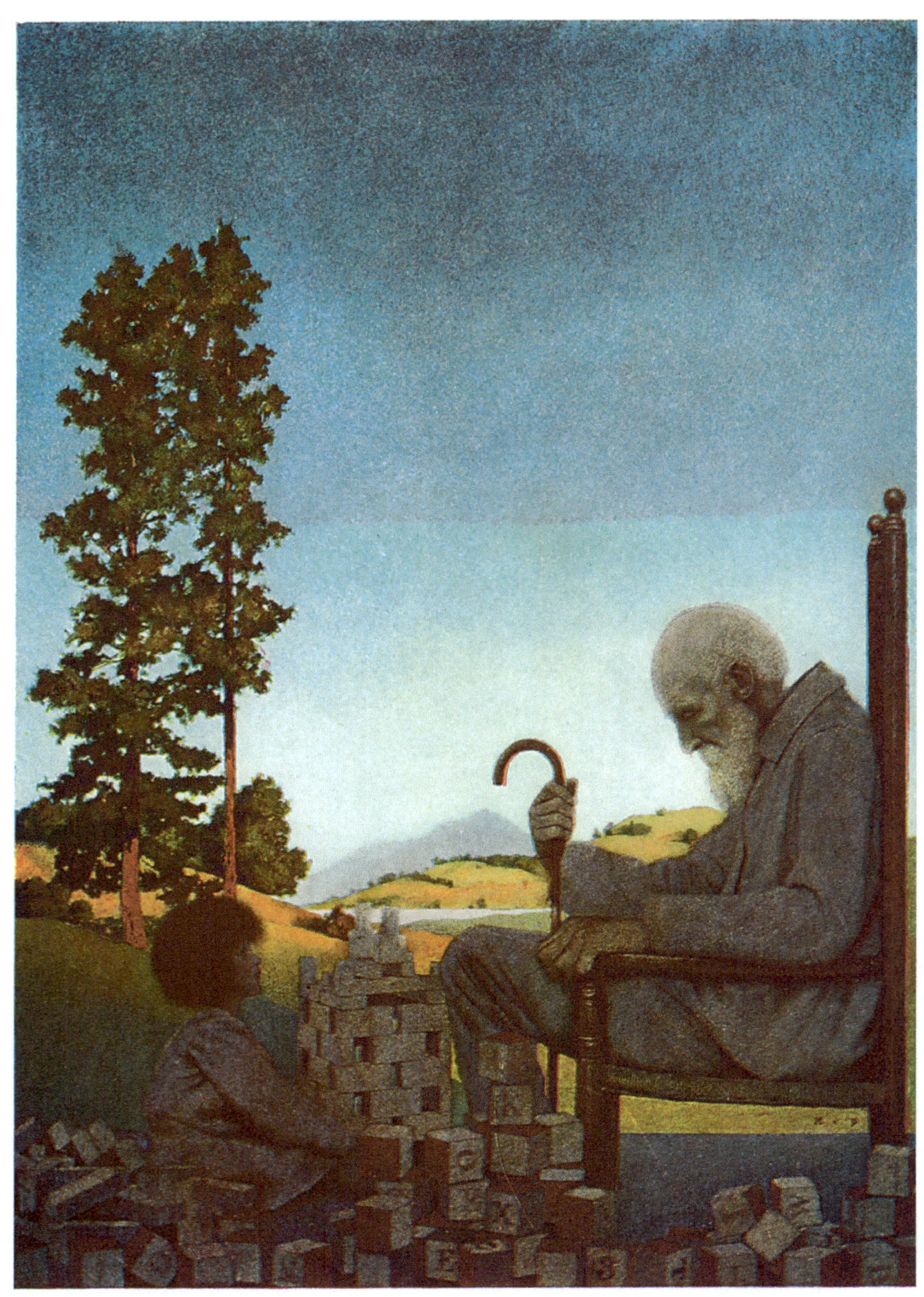

Plate 32.

"Shuffle-Shoon and Amber-Locks"

Shuffle-Shoon and Amber-Locks
Sit together, building blocks;
Shuffle-Shoon is old and gray,
Amber-Locks is a little child.

Poems of Childhood, 1904

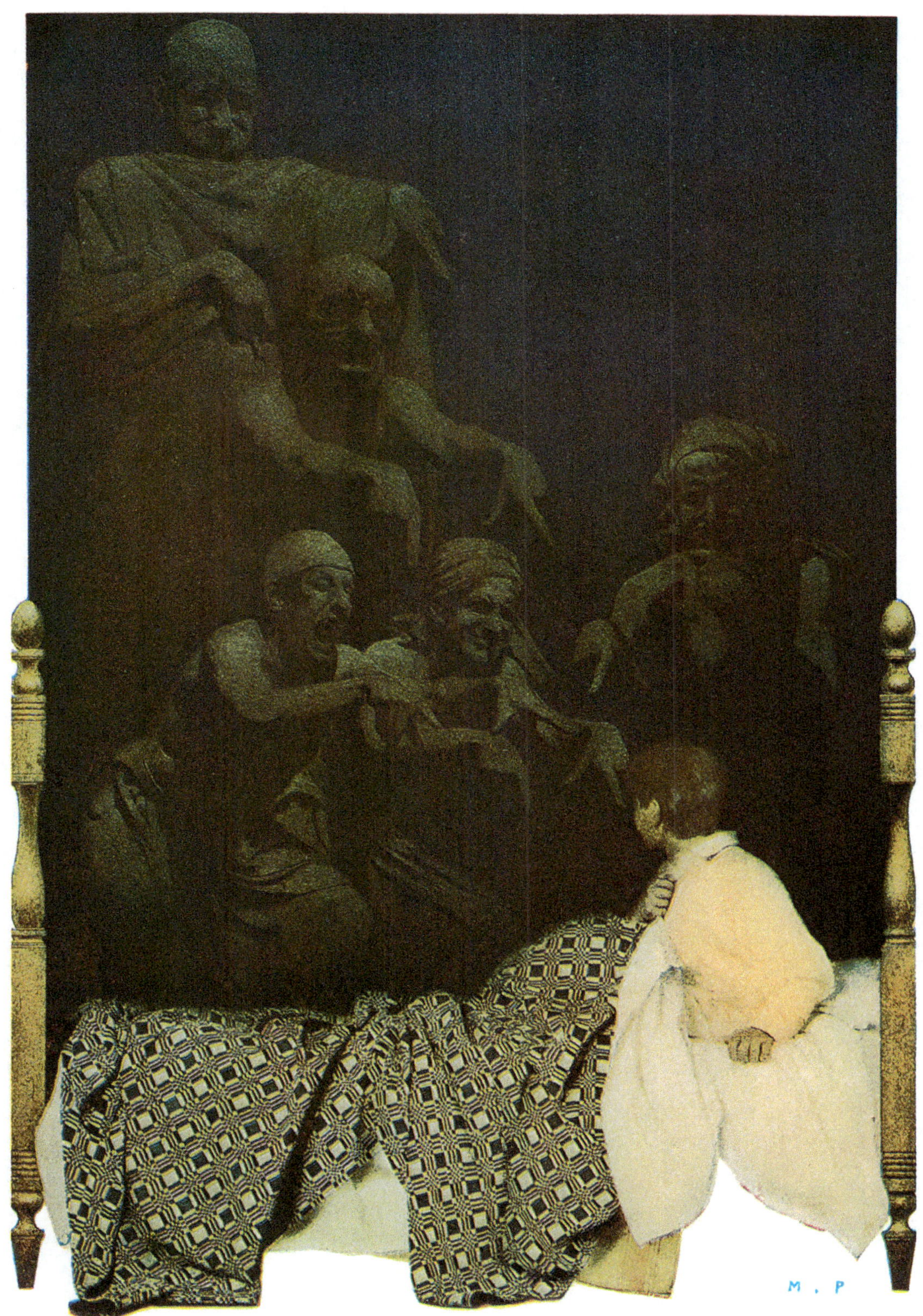

Plate 33.

"Seein' Things"

I woke up in the dark an' saw things standin' in a row,
A-lookin' at me cross-eyed an' p'intin' at me—so!

Poems of Childhood, 1904

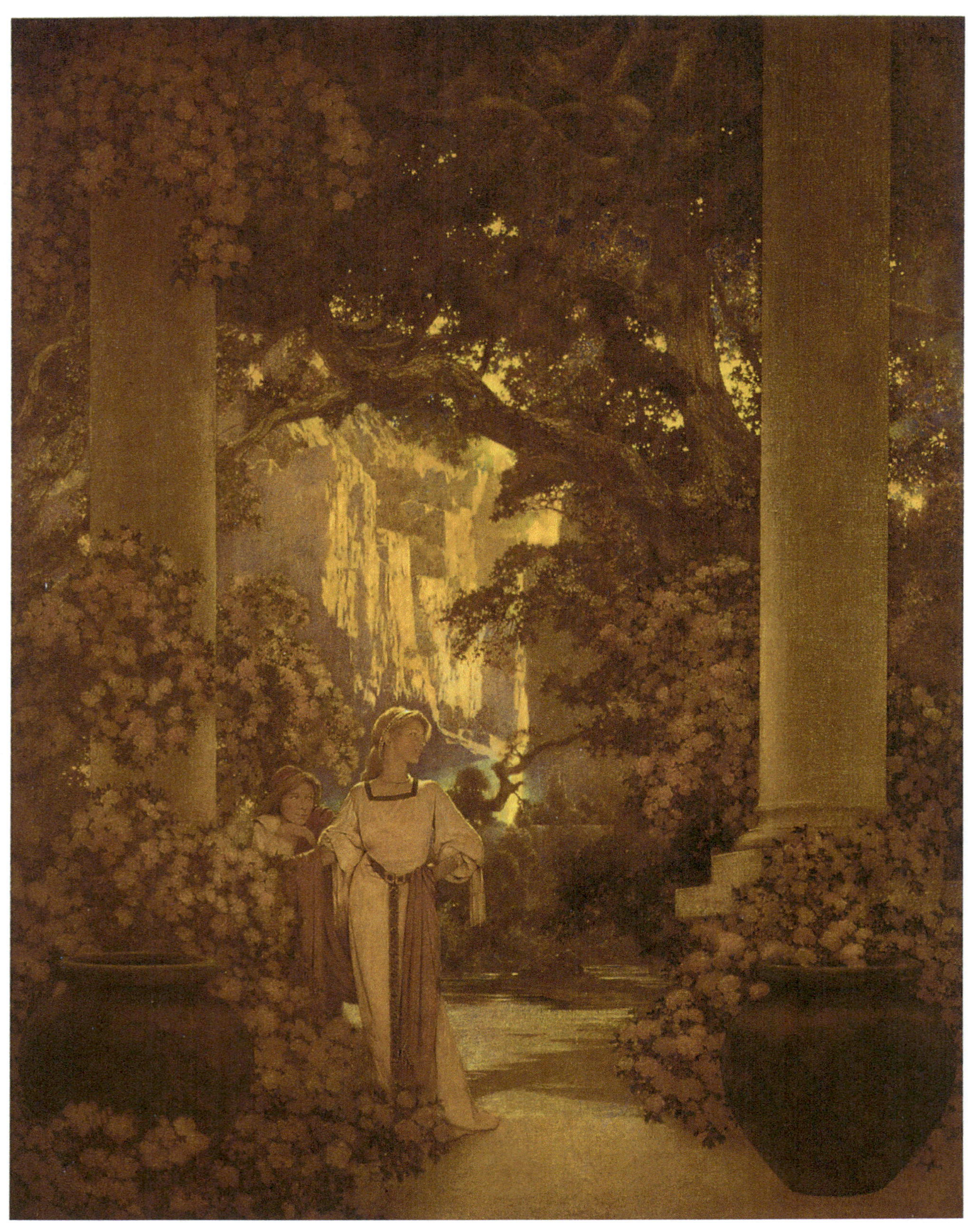

Plate 34.

The Land of Make-Believe (painted in 1905)
Scribner's Magazine, August 1912

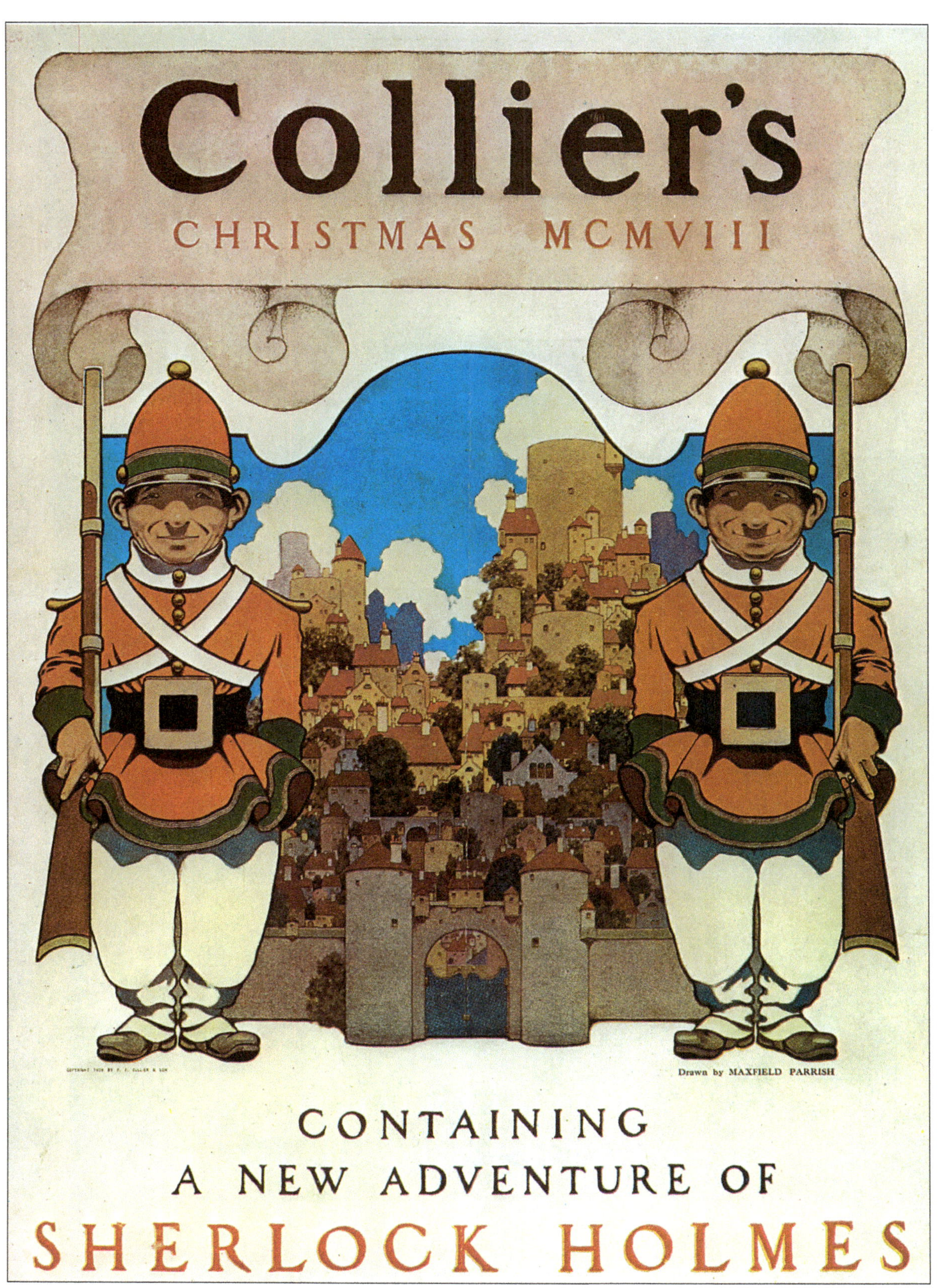

Plate 35.

Cover
Collier's magazine, December 12, 1908

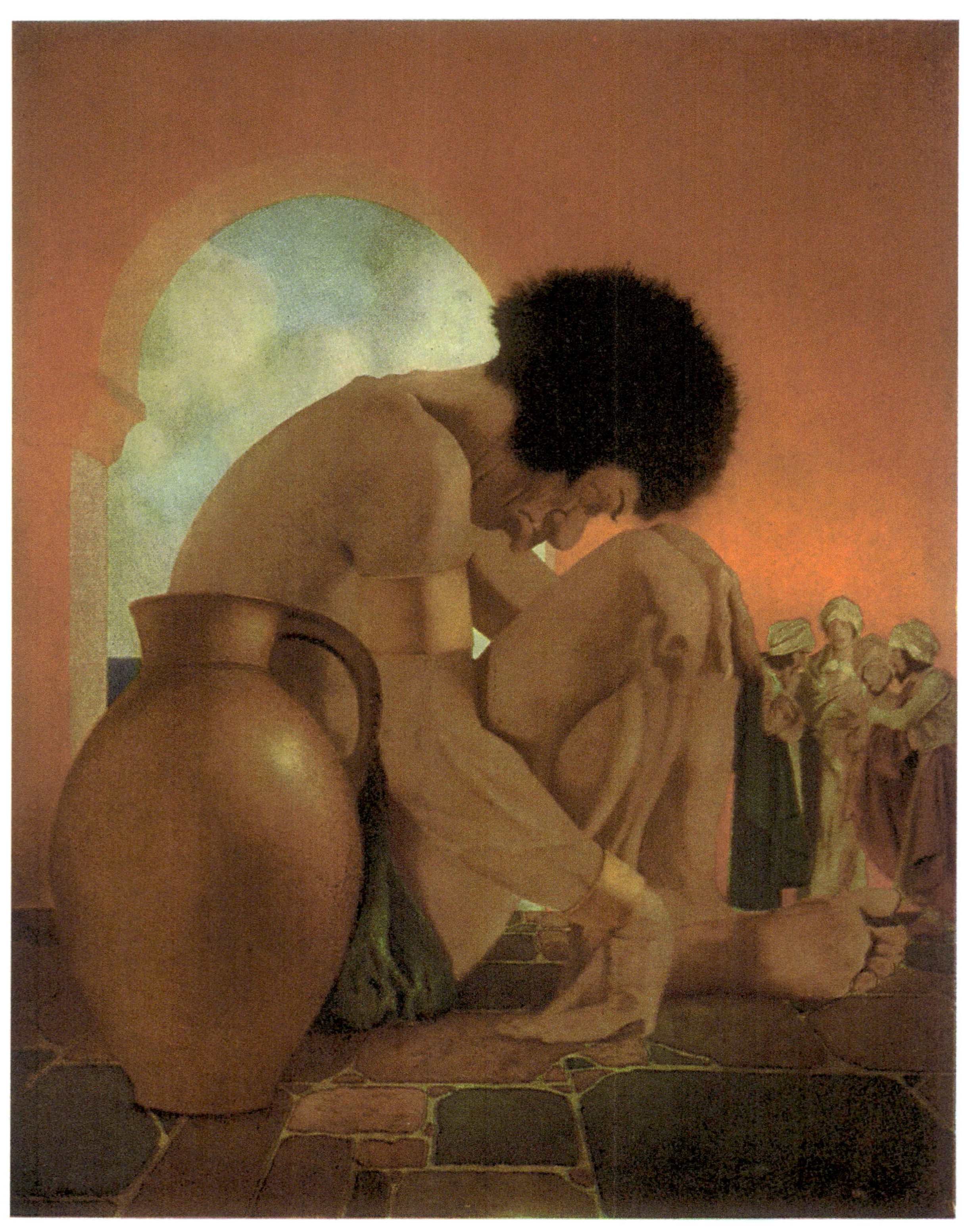

Plate 36.

Sinbad Plots against the Giant
The Arabian Nights: Their Best-Known Tales, 1909

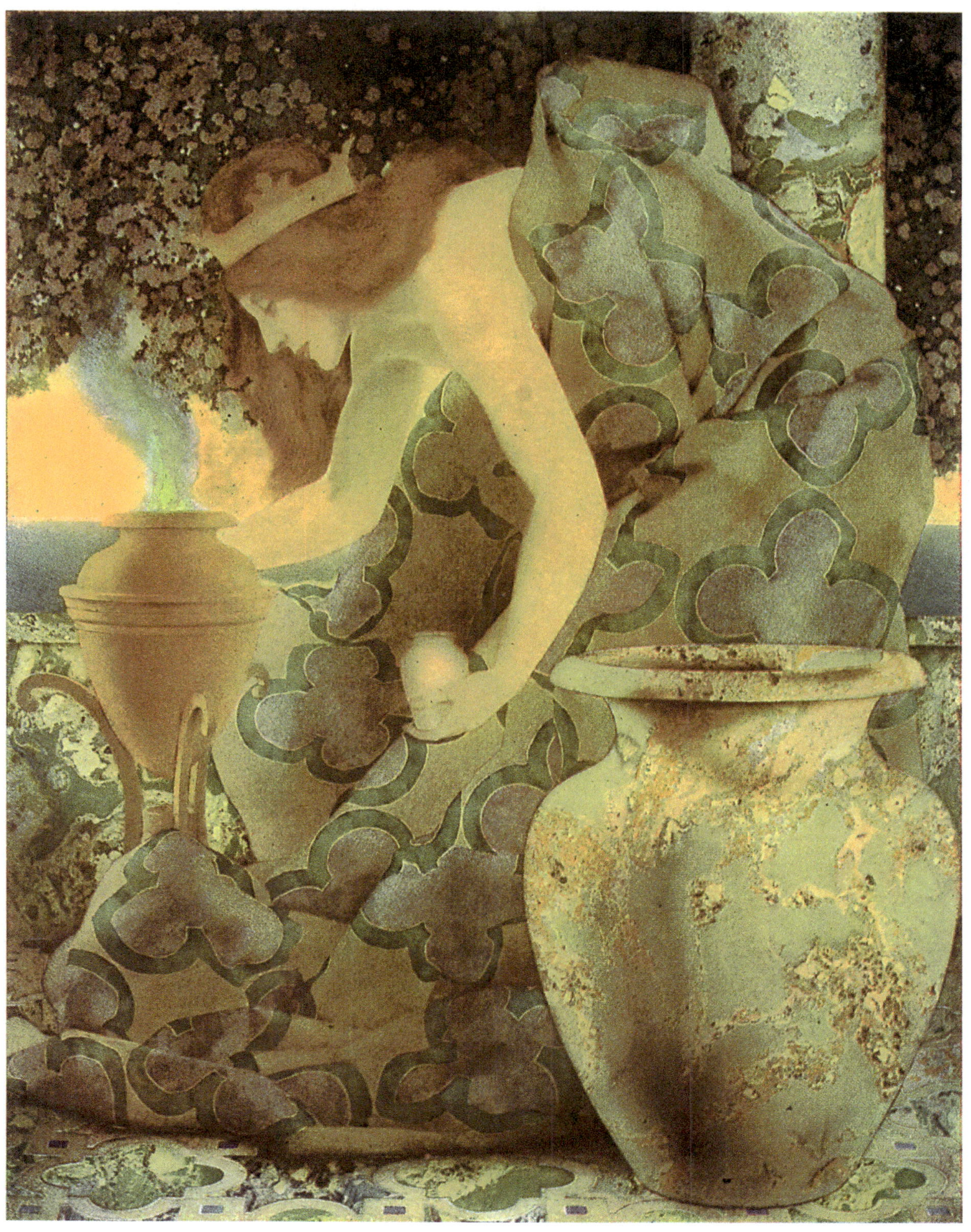

Plate 37.

Gulnare of the Sea
The Arabian Nights: Their Best-Known Tales, 1909

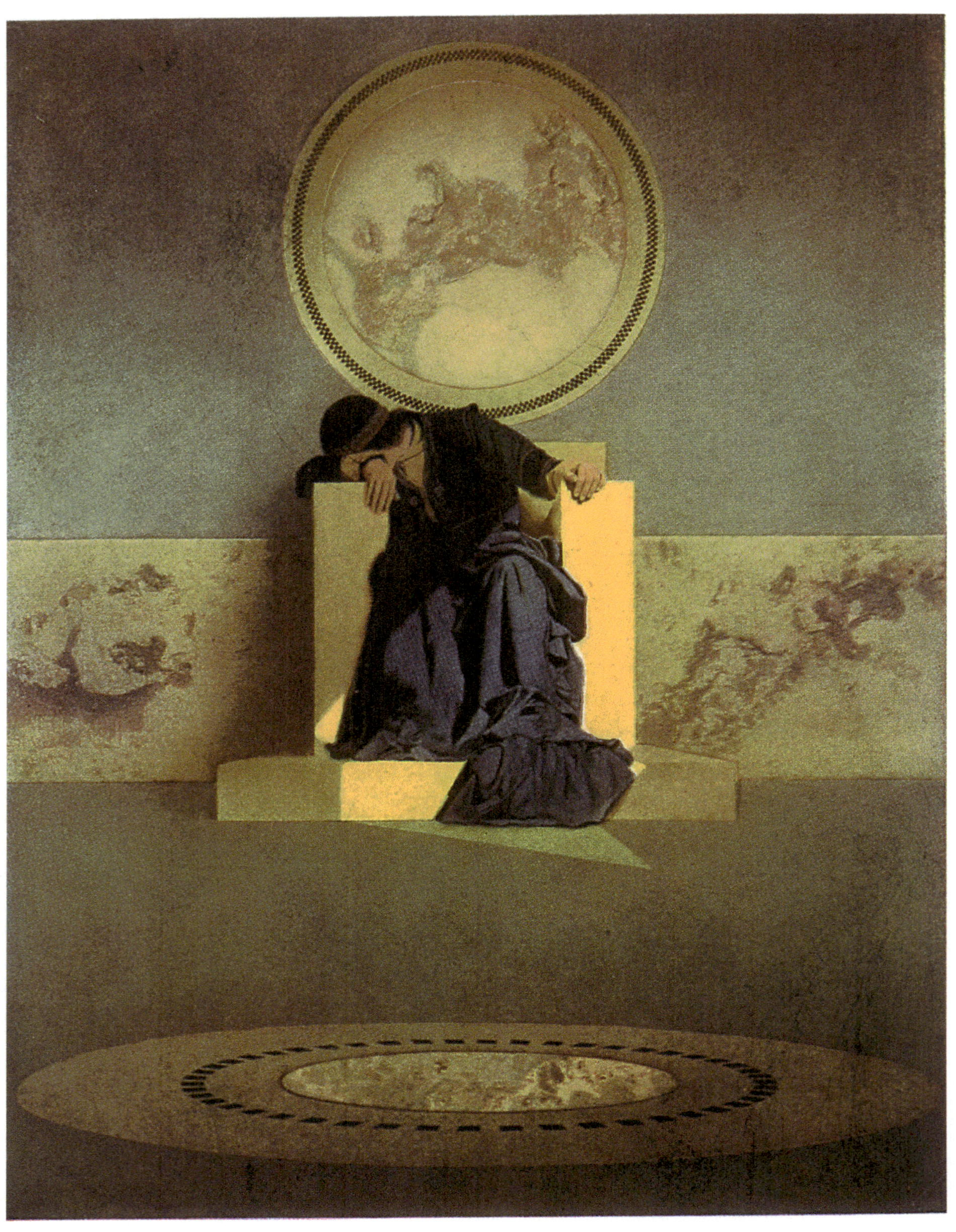

Plate 38.

The Young King of the Black Isles
The Arabian Nights: Their Best-Known Tales, 1909

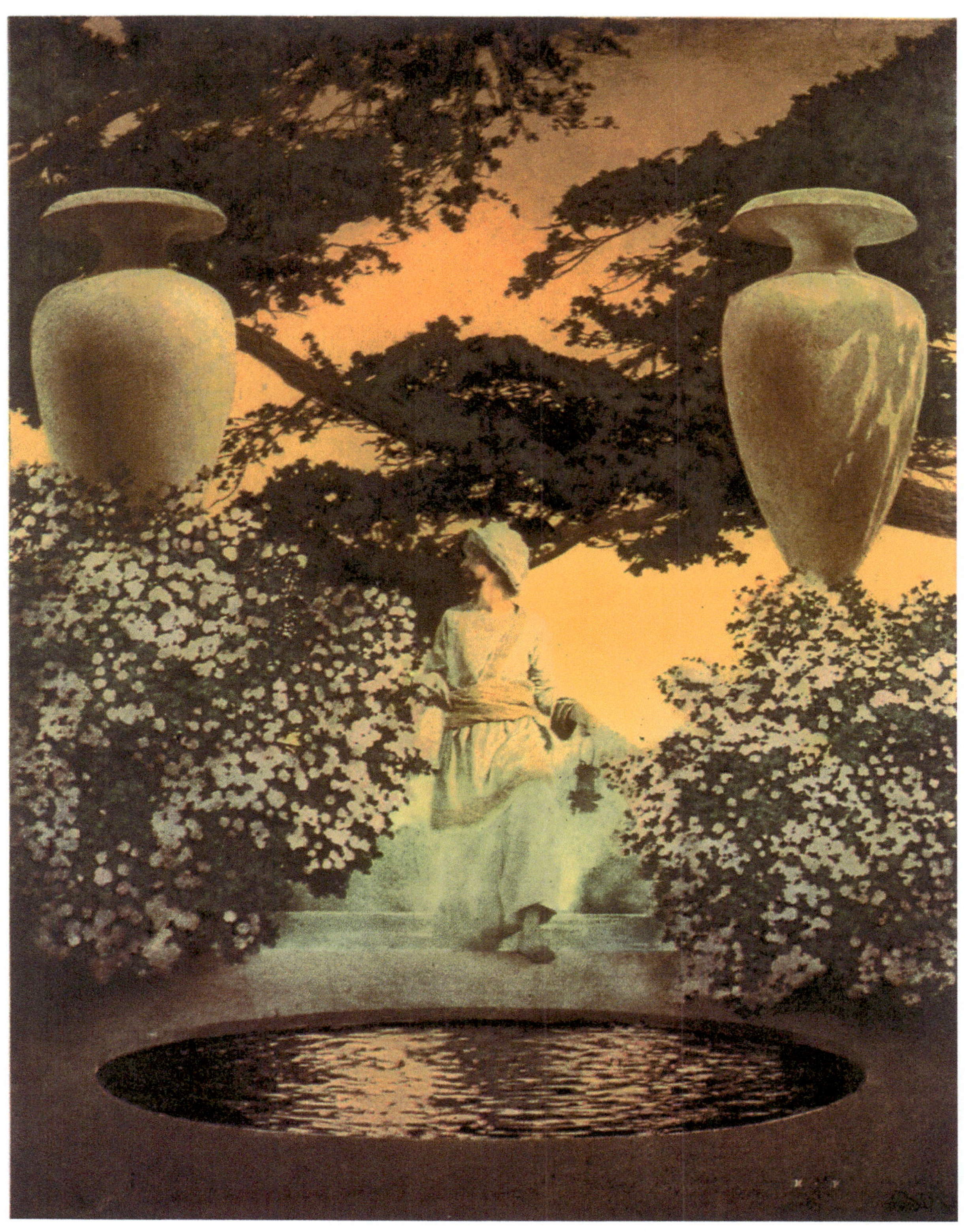

Plate 39.

The Story of the King's Son
The Arabian Nights: Their Best-Known Tales, 1909

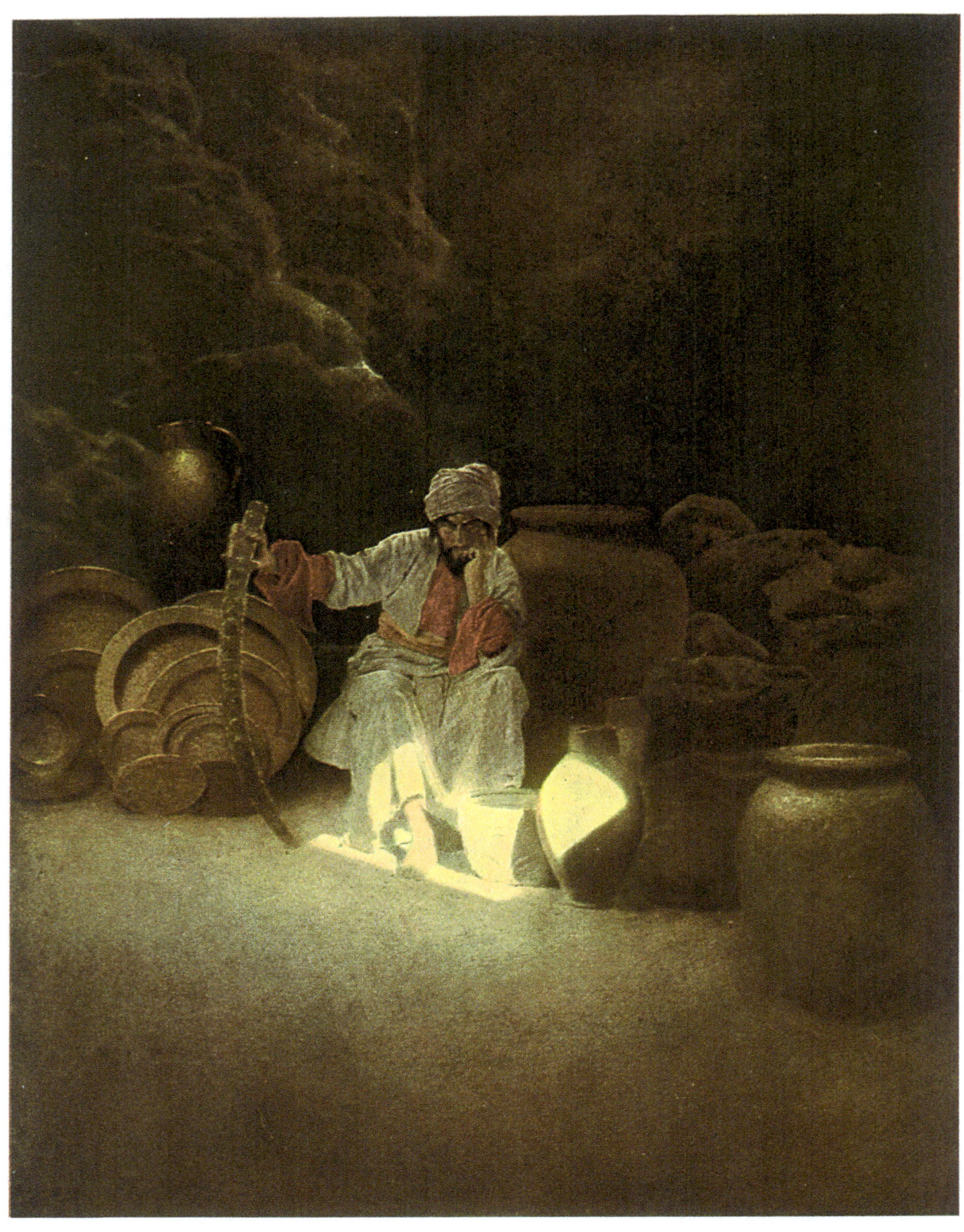

Plate 40.

Cassim in the Cave of the Forty Thieves
The Arabian Nights: Their Best-Known Tales, 1909

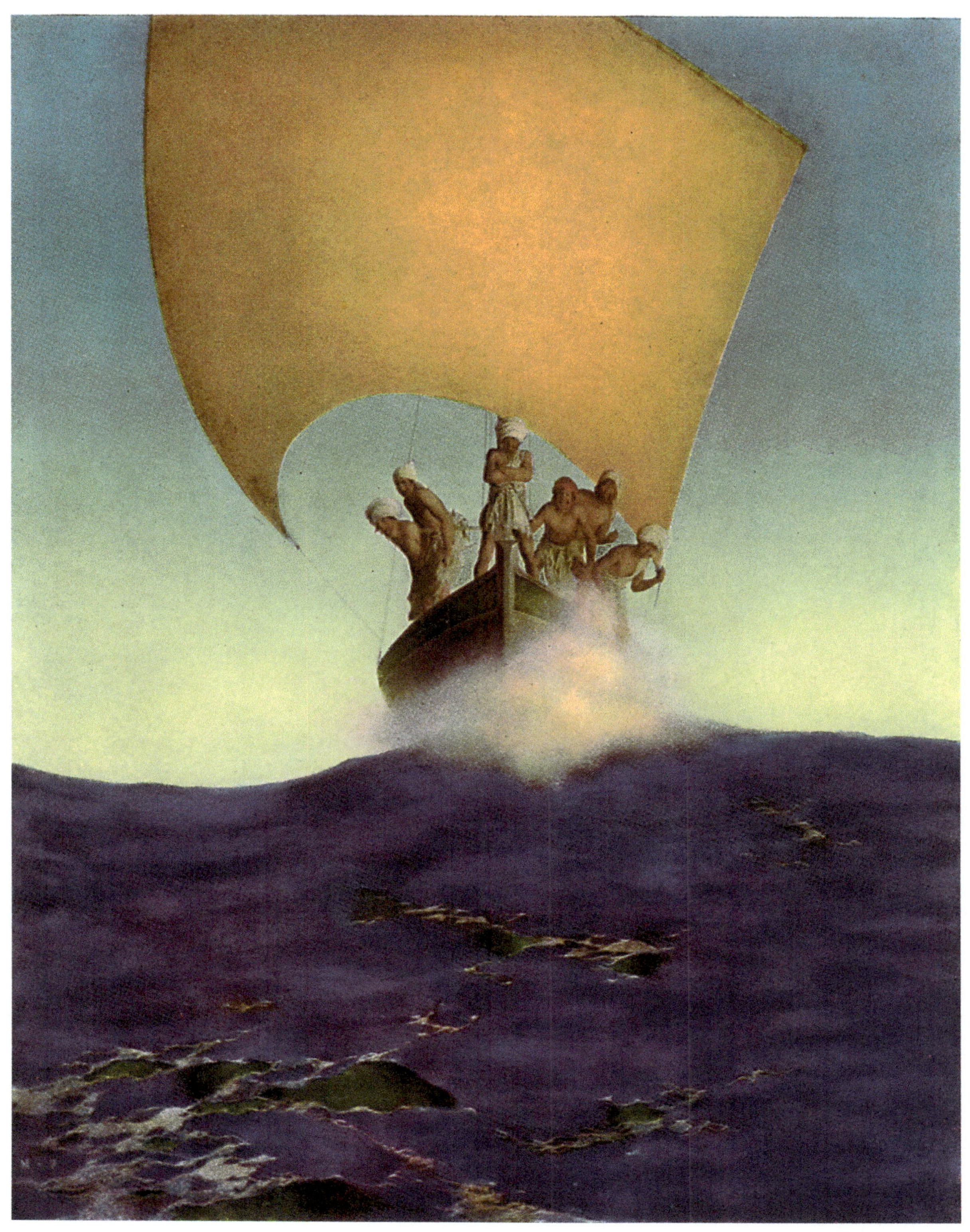

Plate 41.

The History of Codadad and His Brothers

The Arabian Nights: Their Best-Known Tales, 1909

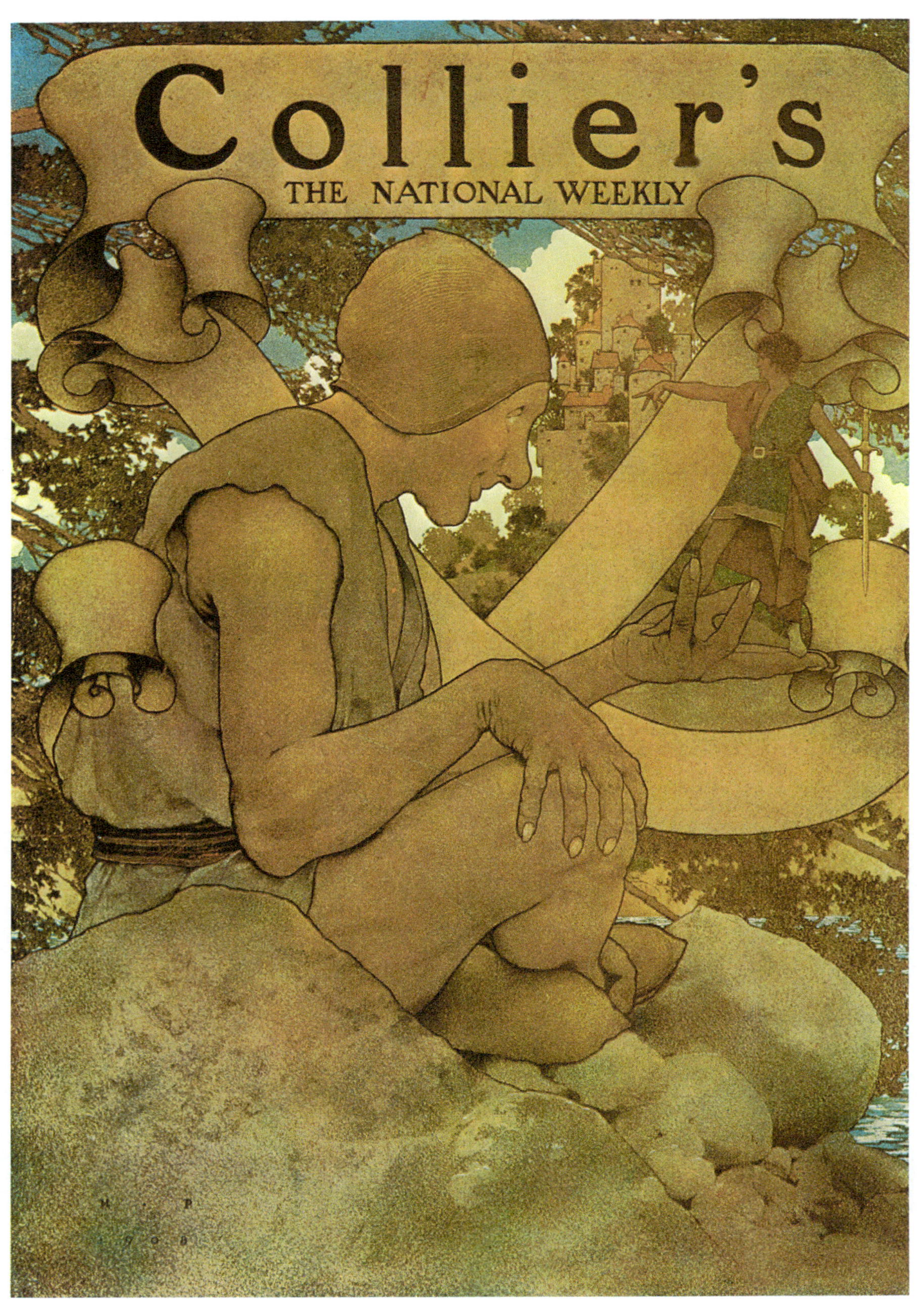

Plate 42.

Cover
Collier's magazine, July 30, 1910

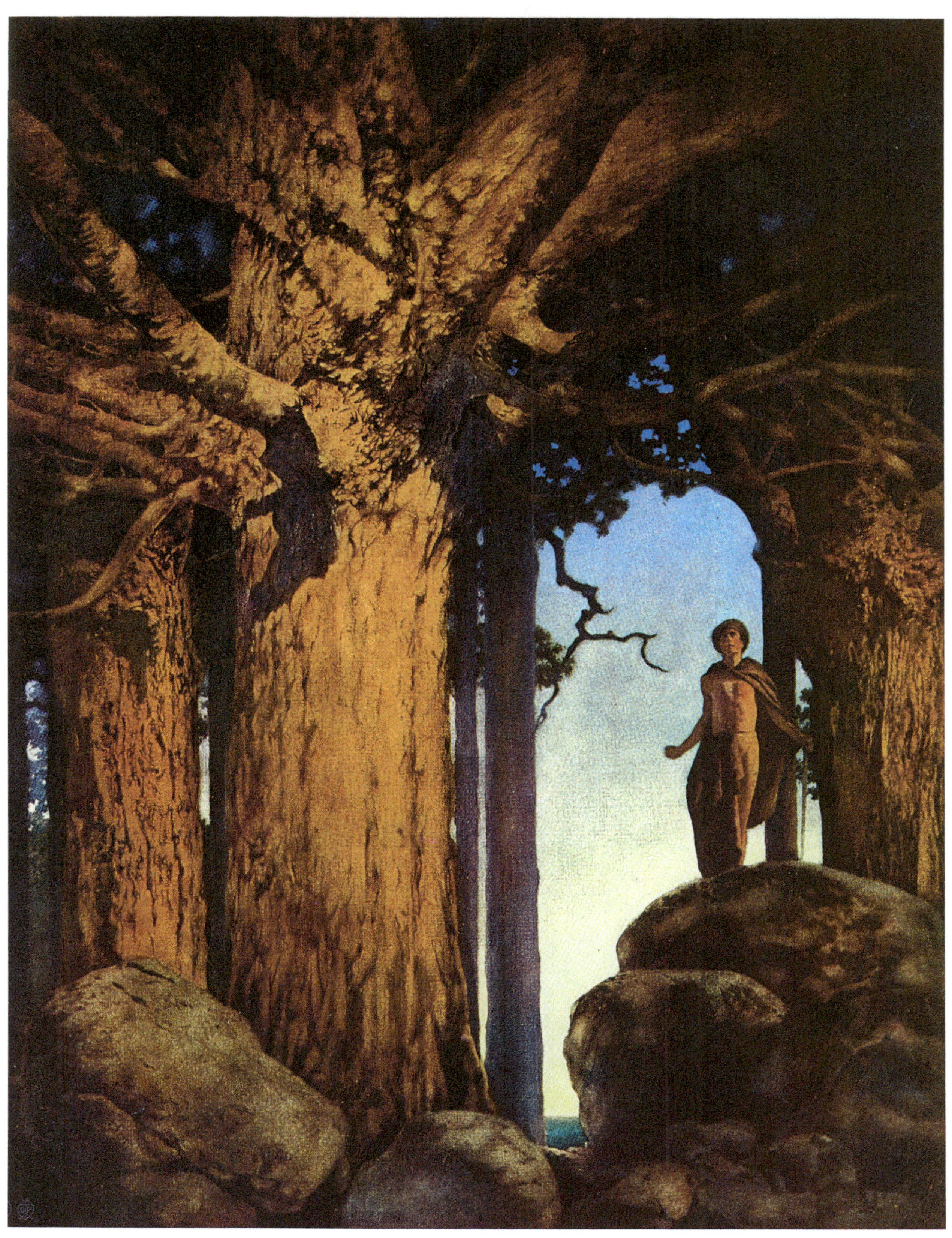

Plate 43.

Jason and the Talking Oak
Tanglewood Tales, 1910

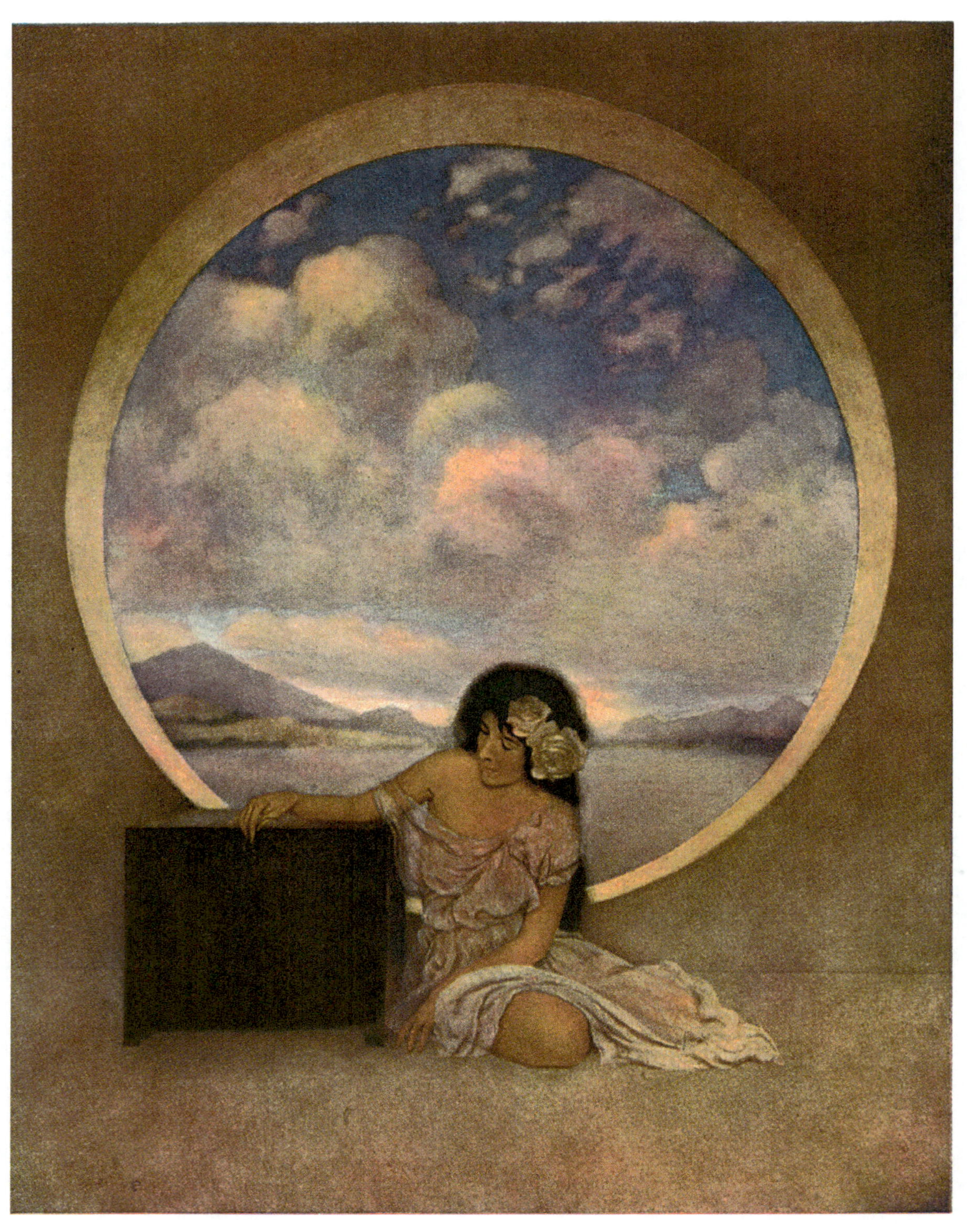

Plate 44.

Pandora
Tanglewood Tales, 1910

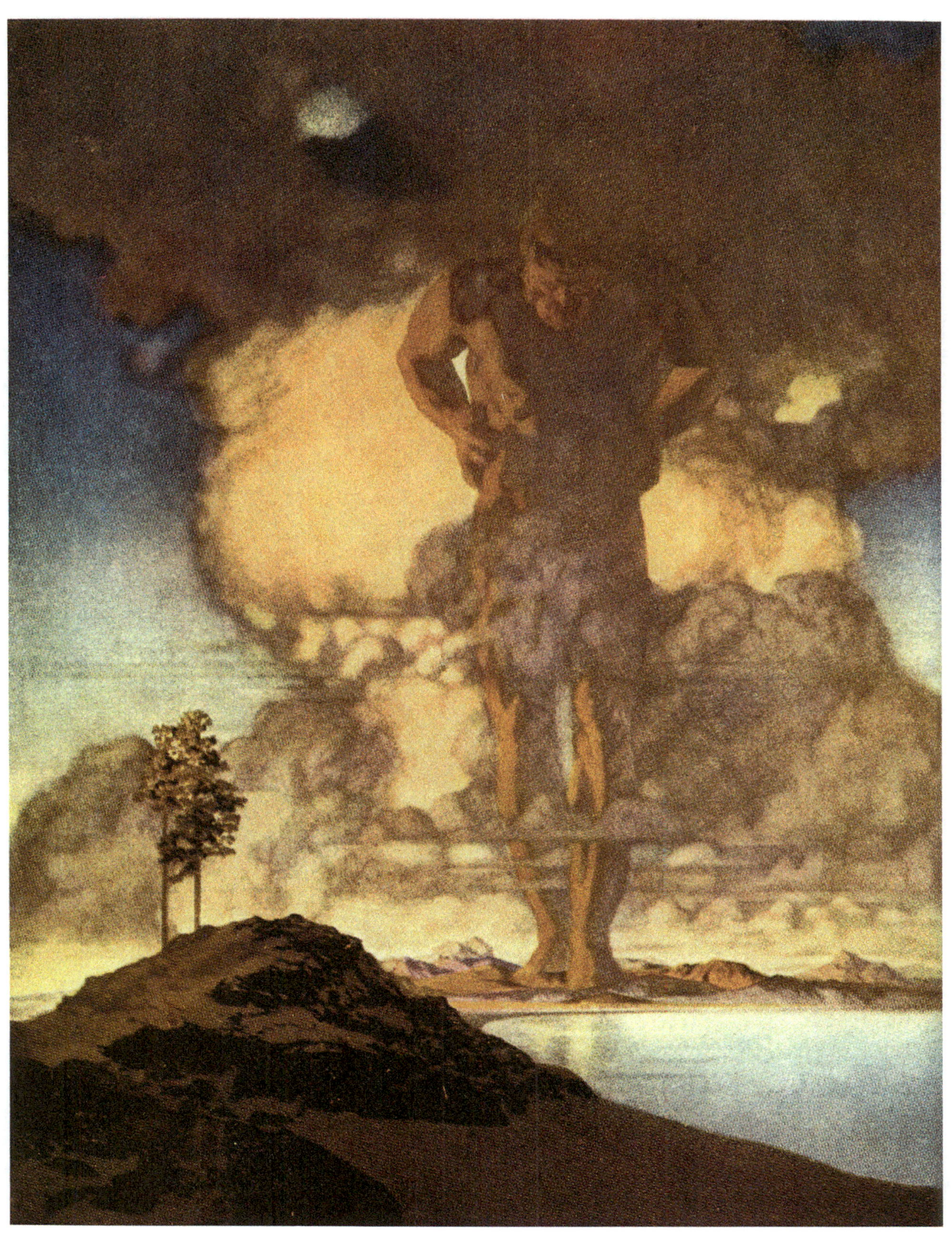

Plate 45.

Atlas

Tanglewood Tales, 1910

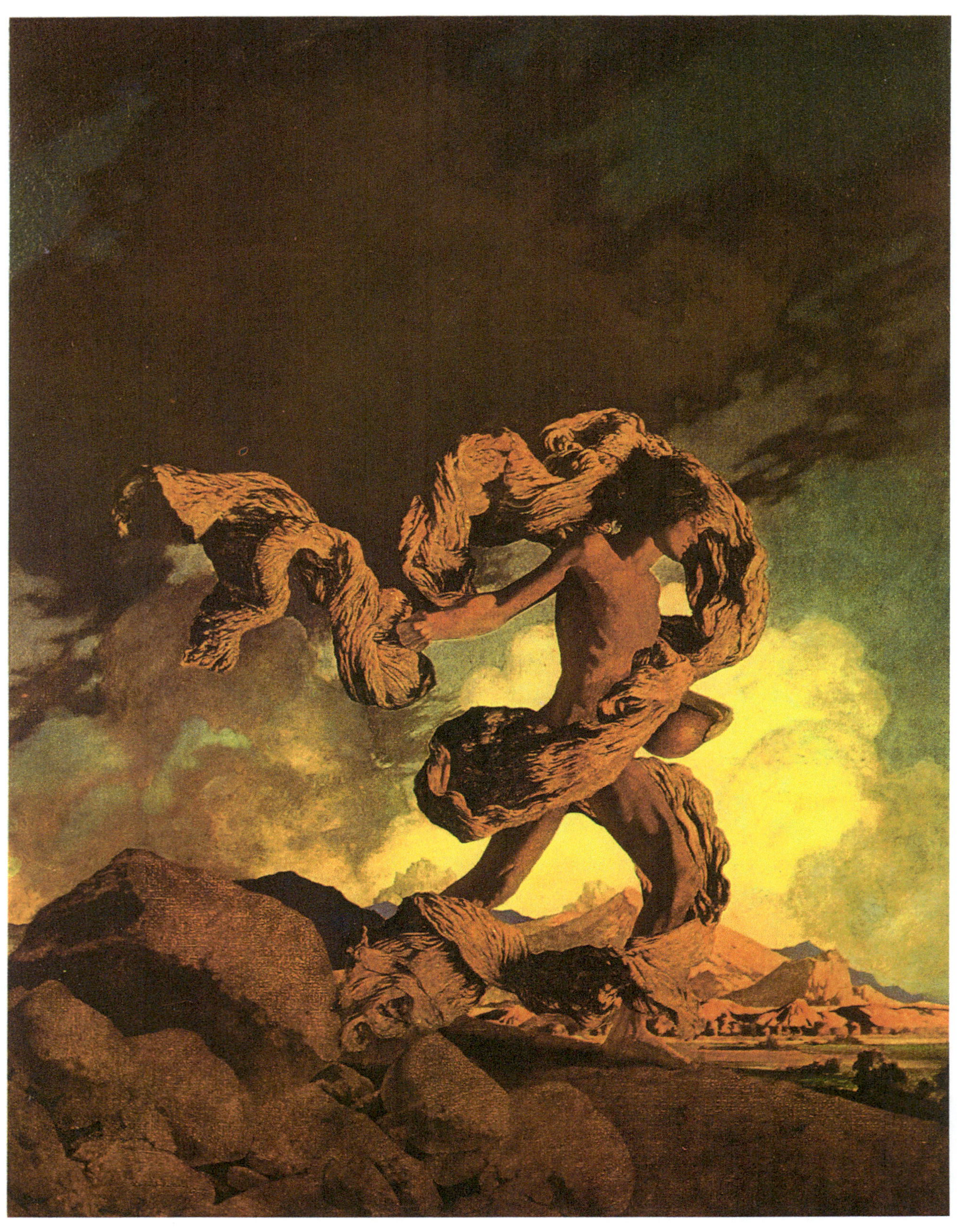

Plate 46.

Cadmus Sowing the Dragon's Teeth
Tanglewood Tales, 1910

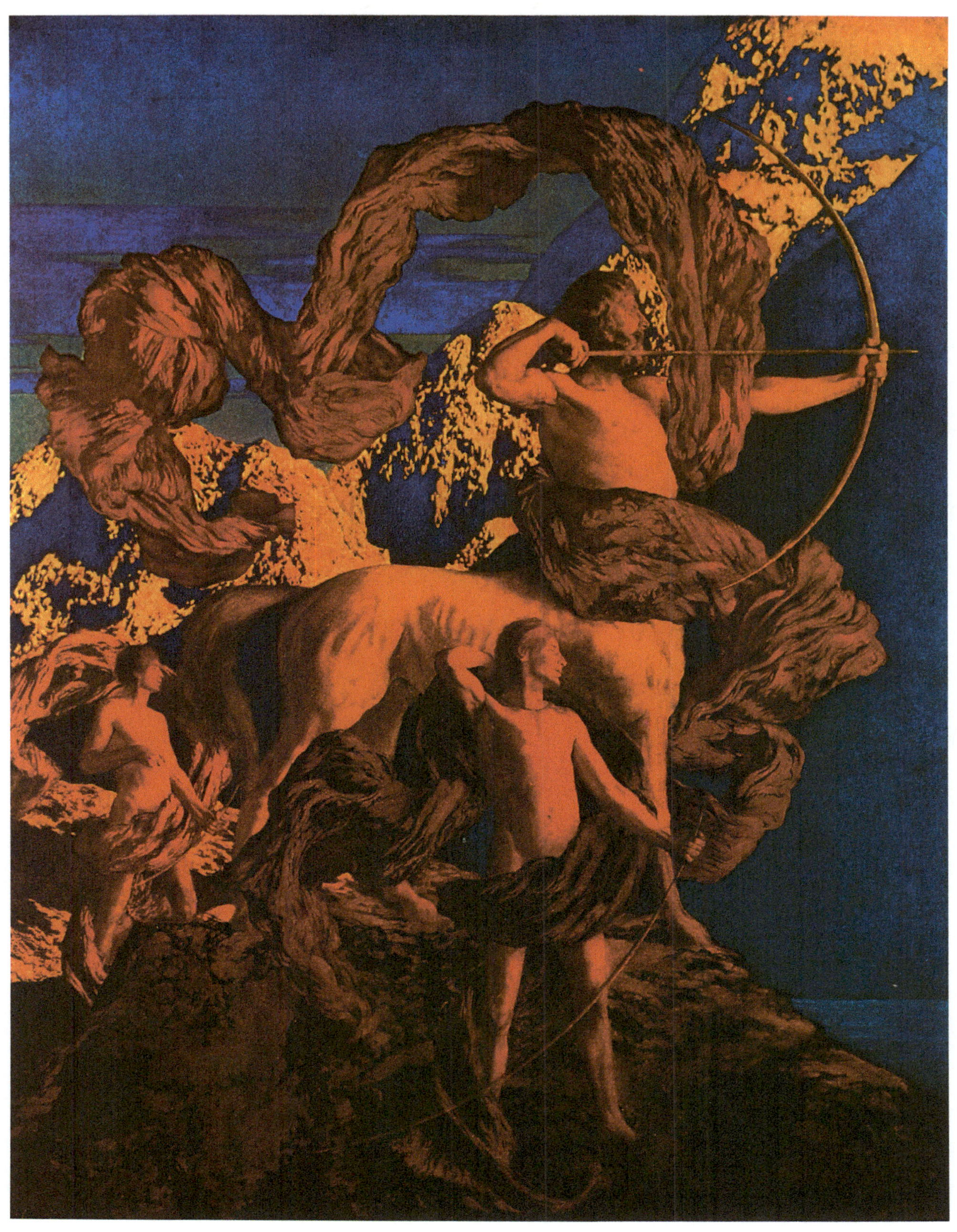

Plate 47.

Jason and His Teacher
Tanglewood Tales, 1910

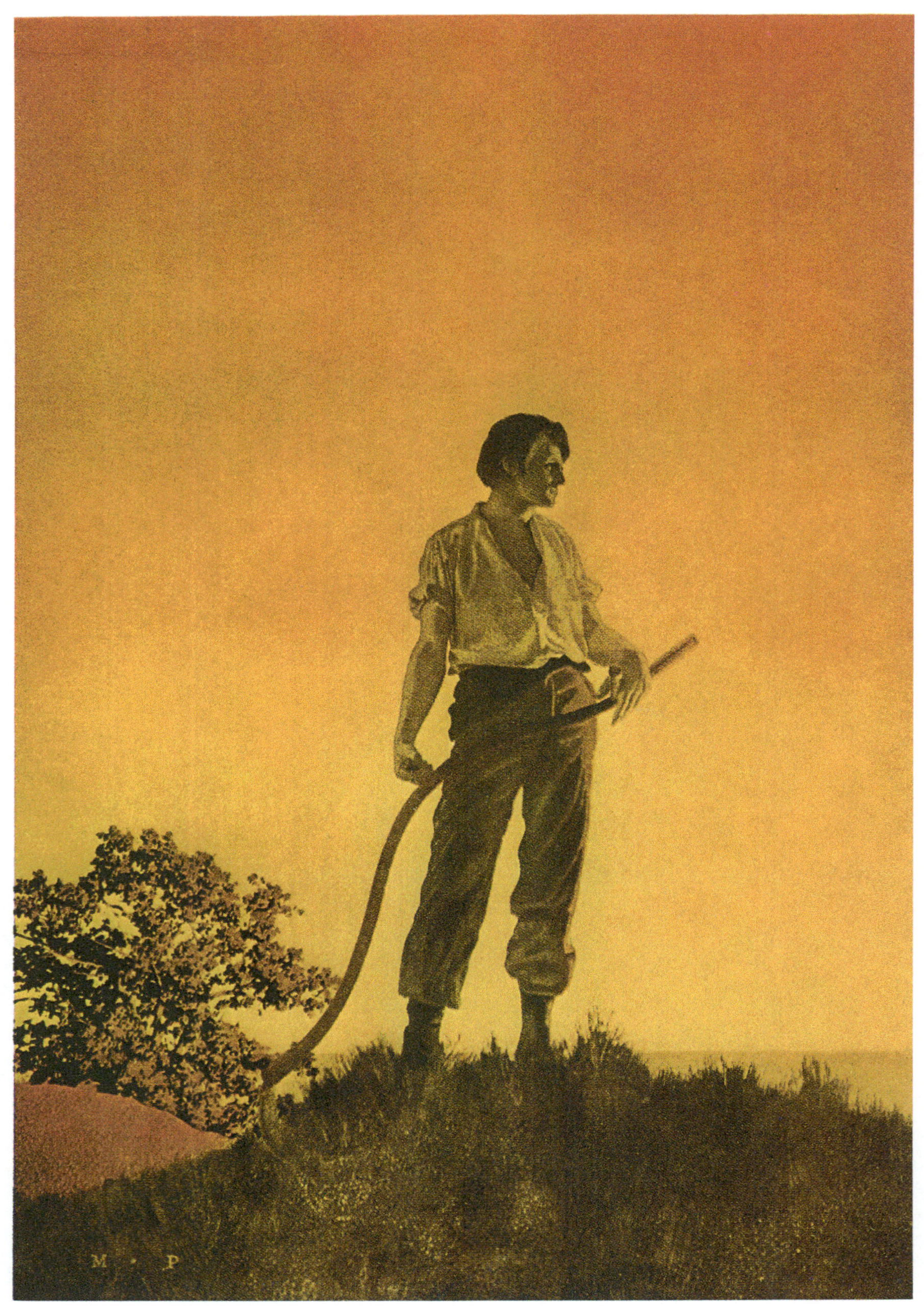

Plate 48.

Harvest

The Golden Treasury of Songs and Lyrics, 1911

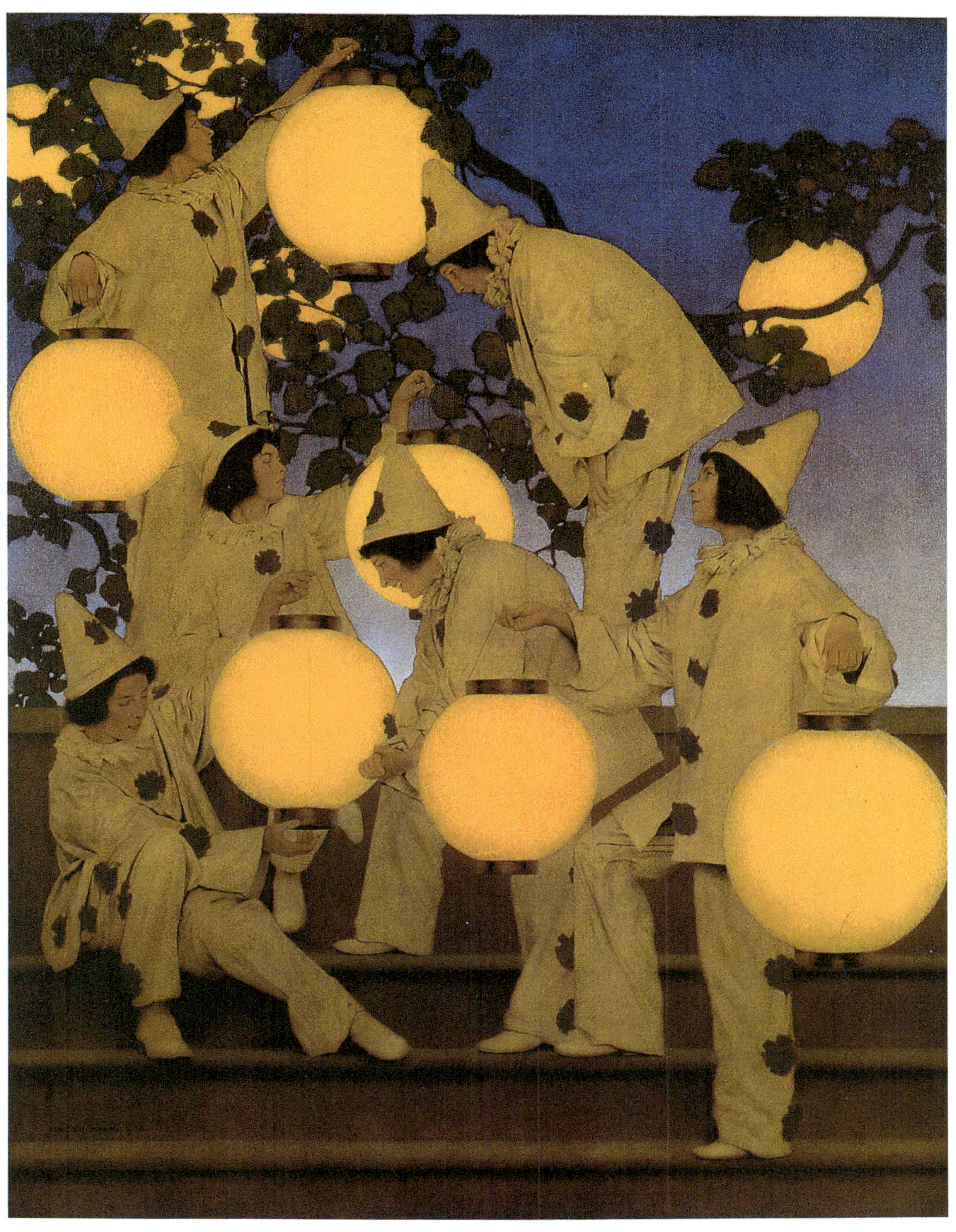

Plate 49.

The Lantern Bearers

The Golden Treasury of Songs and Lyrics, 1911

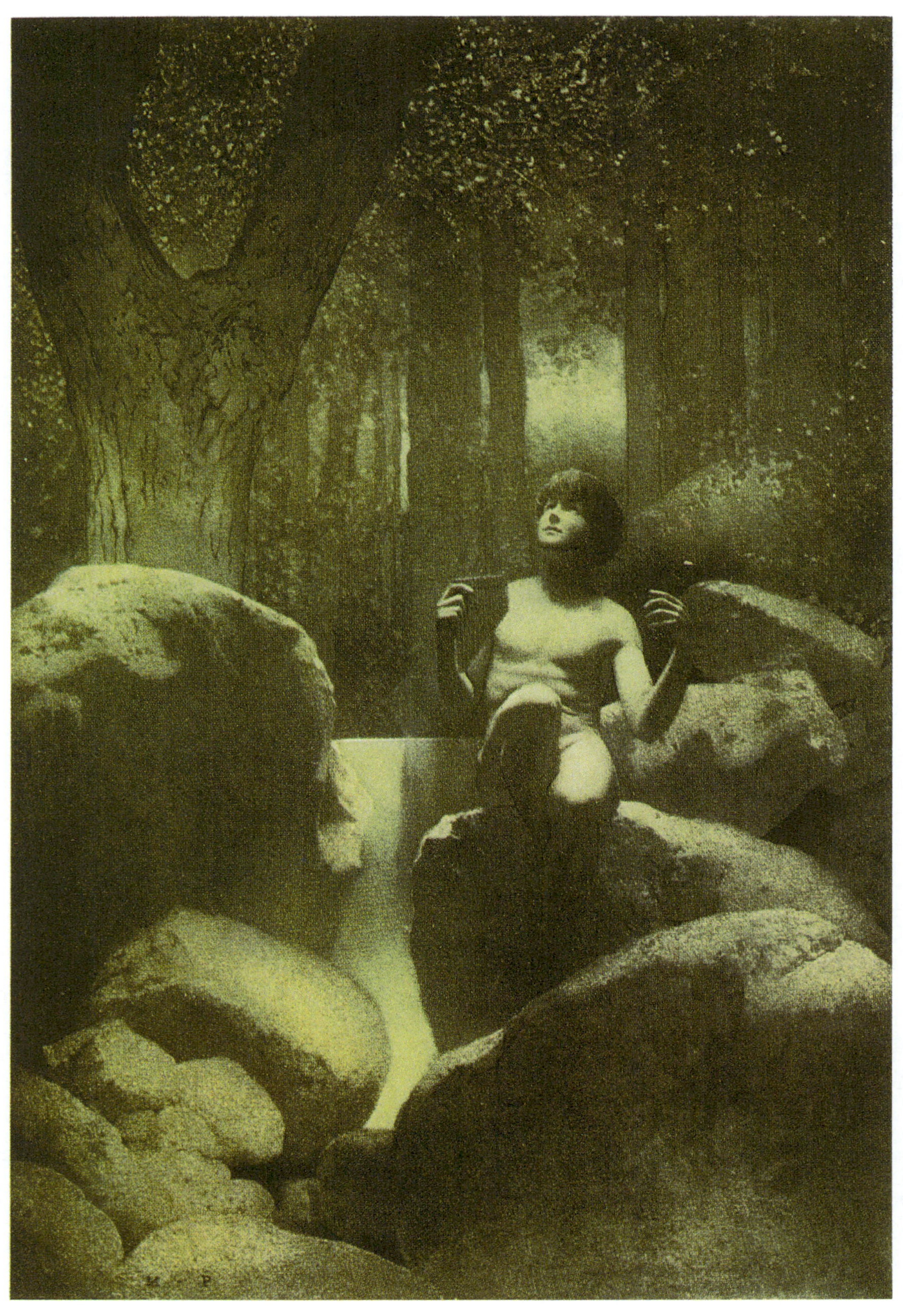

Plate 50.

Summer

The Golden Treasury of Songs and Lyrics, 1911

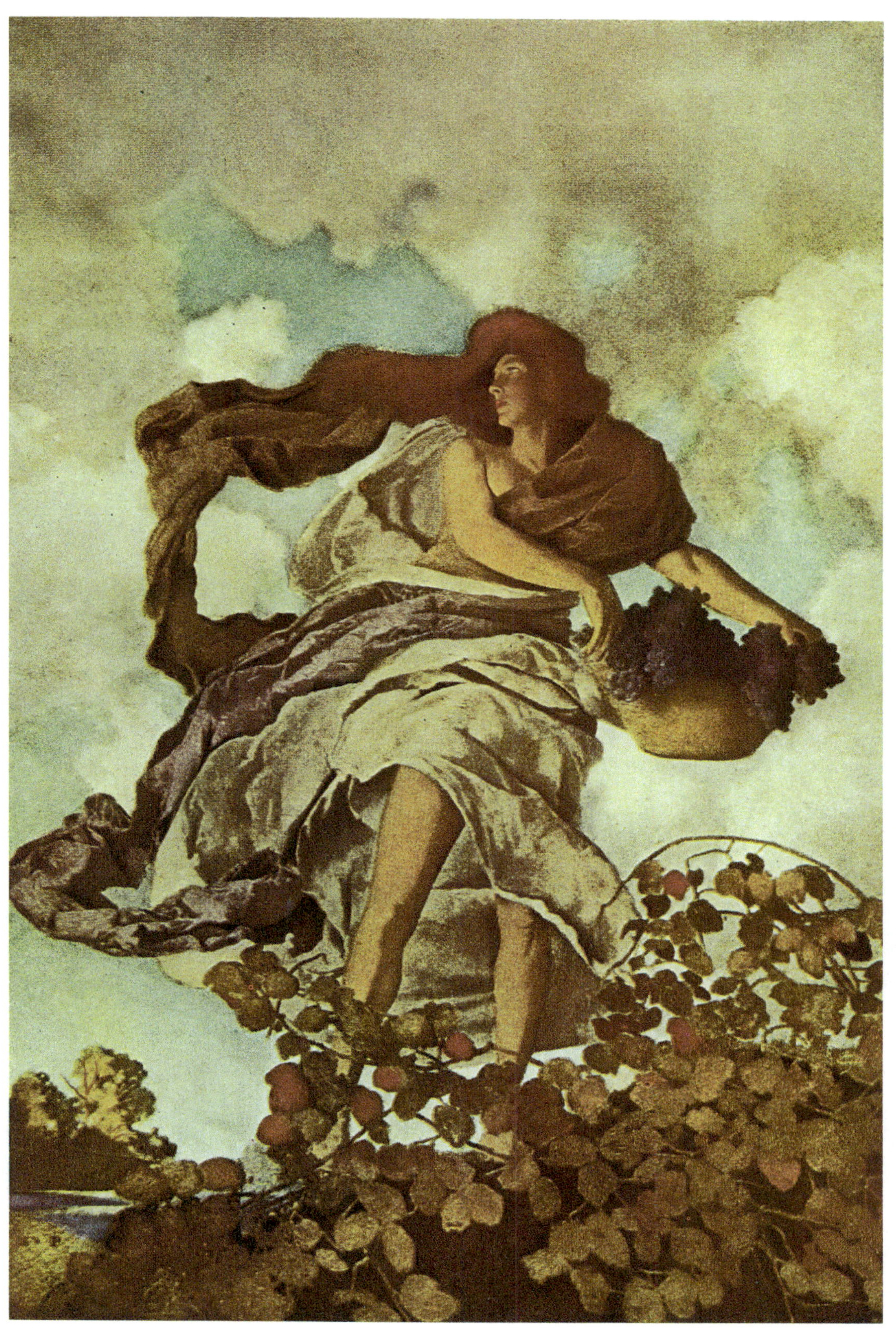

Plate 51.

Autumn

The Golden Treasury of Songs and Lyrics, 1911

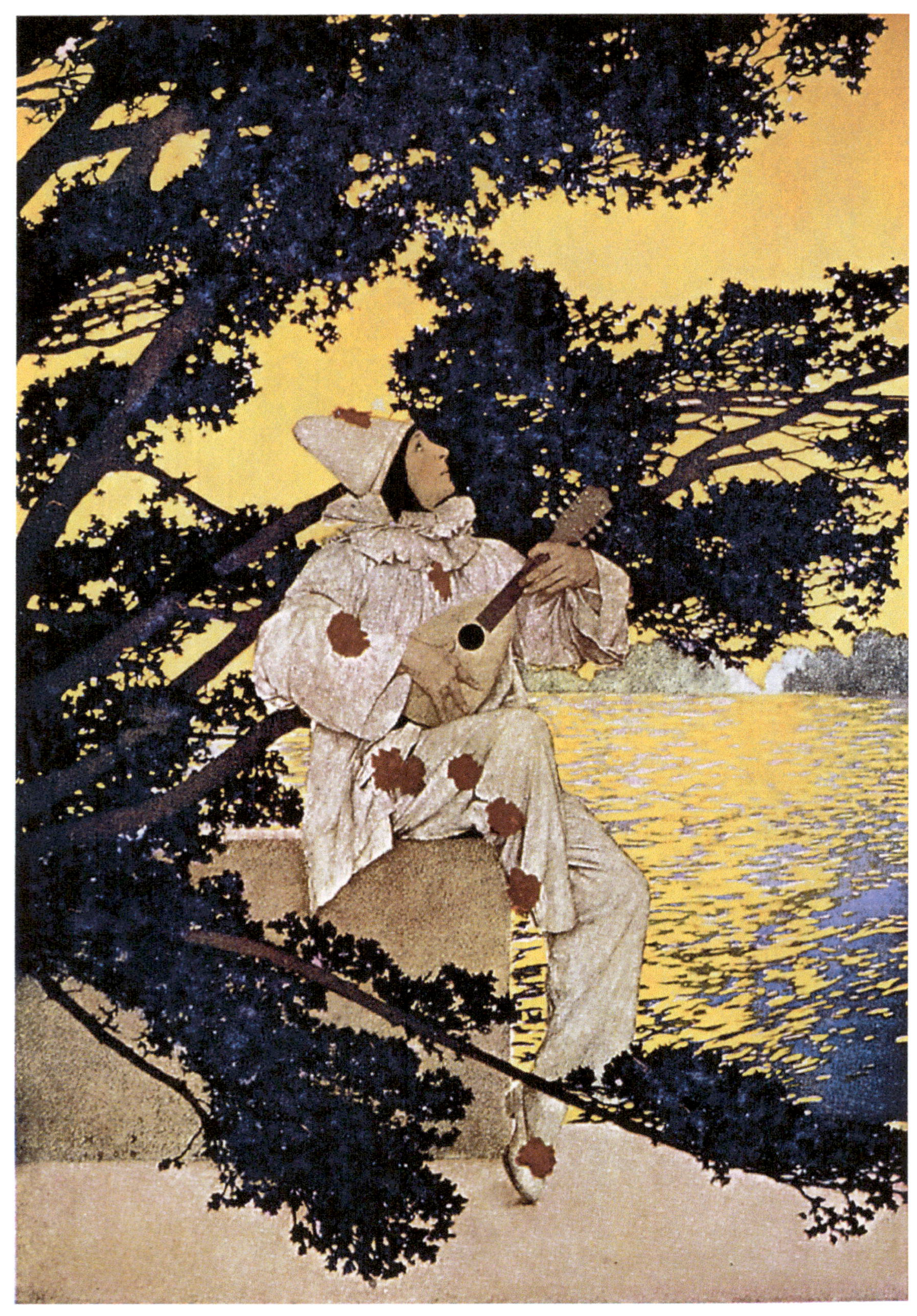

Plate 52.

Pierrot

The Golden Treasury of Songs and Lyrics, 1911

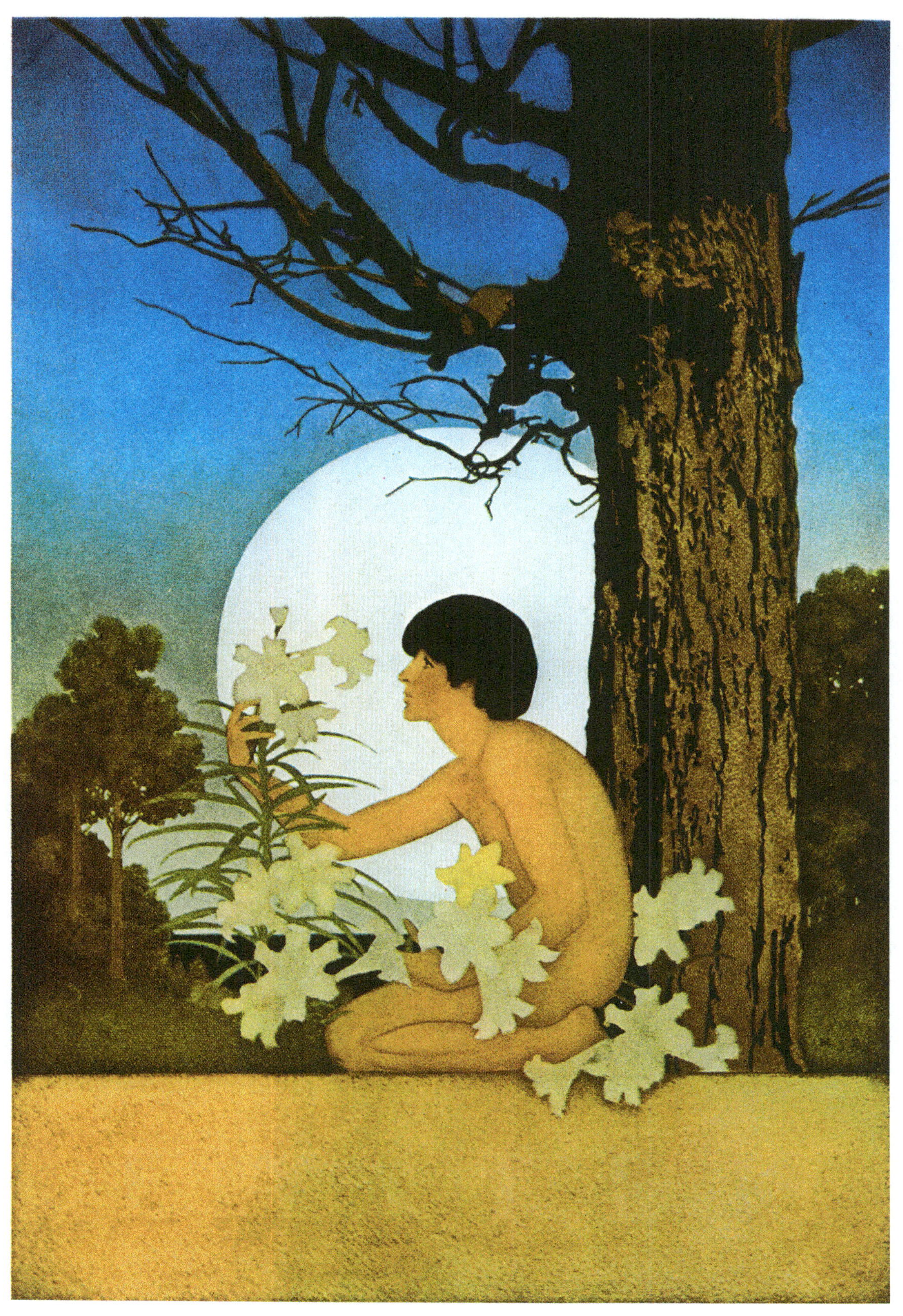

Plate 53.

Easter

The Golden Treasury of Songs and Lyrics, 1911

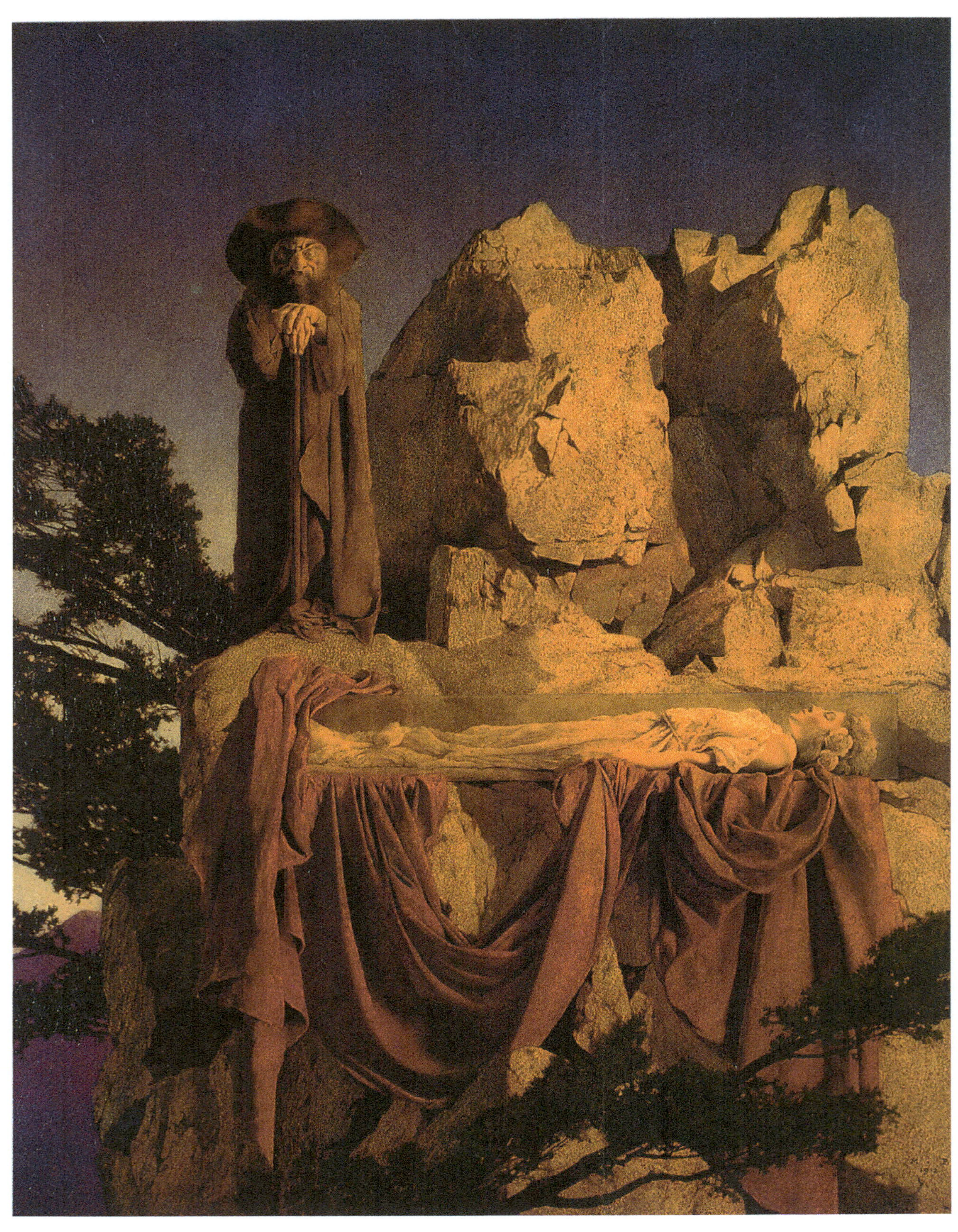

Plate 54.

The Story of Snow Drop
Cover, *Hearst's Magazine*, August 1912

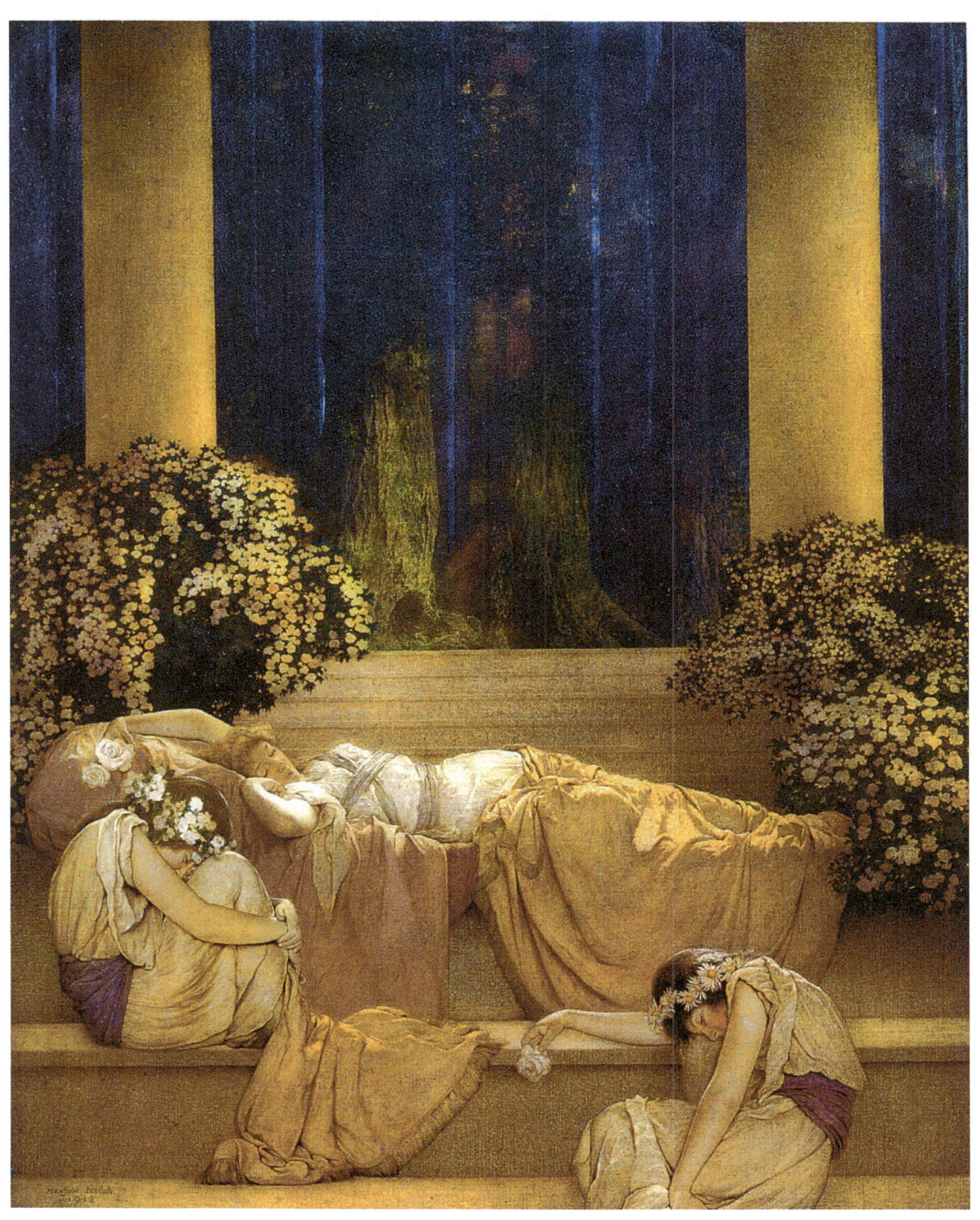

Plate 55.

The Sleeping Beauty
Cover, *Hearst's Magazine,* November 1912

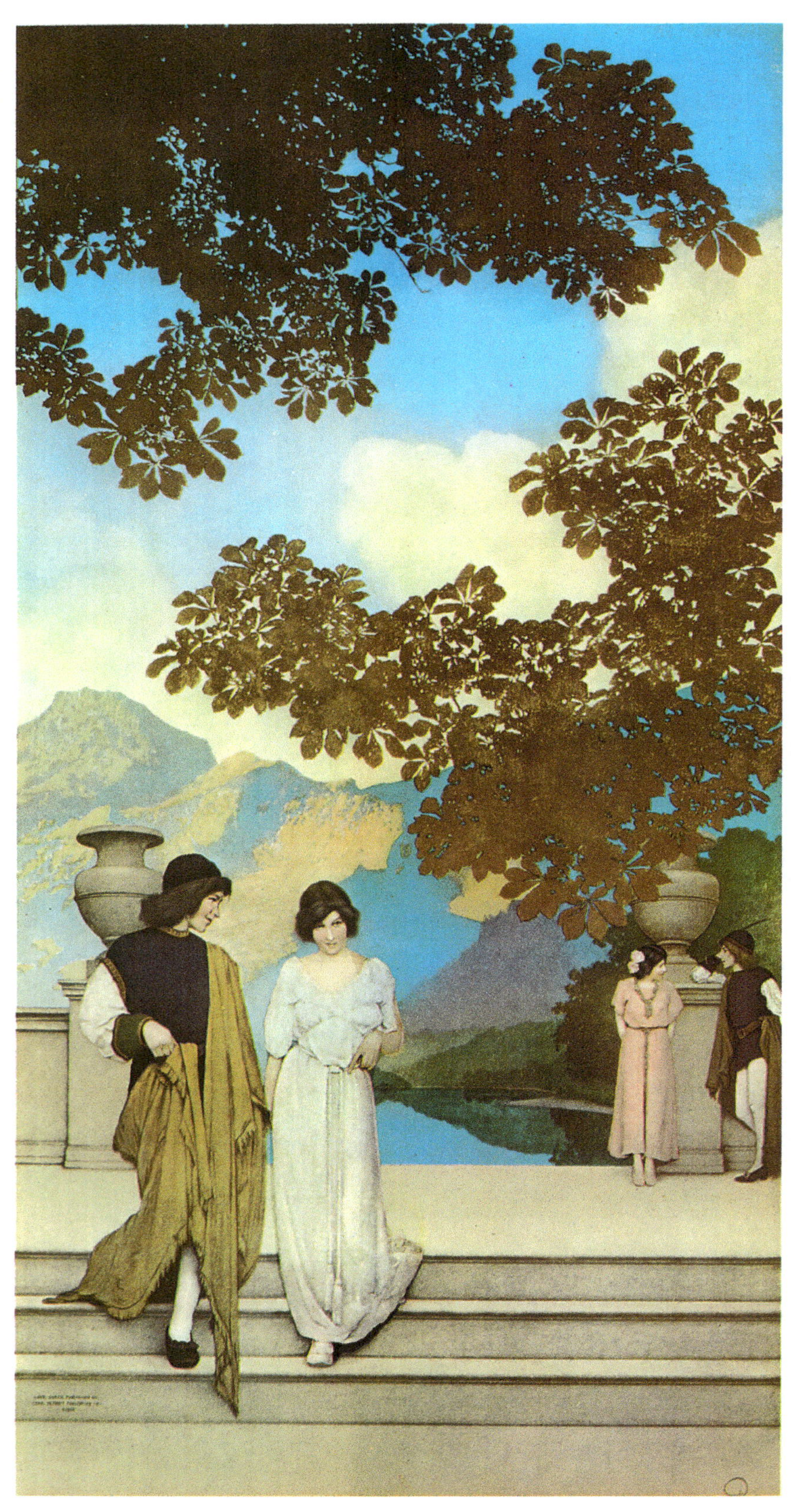

Plate 56.

Panel
The Curtis Publishing Company Mural, 1912–1915

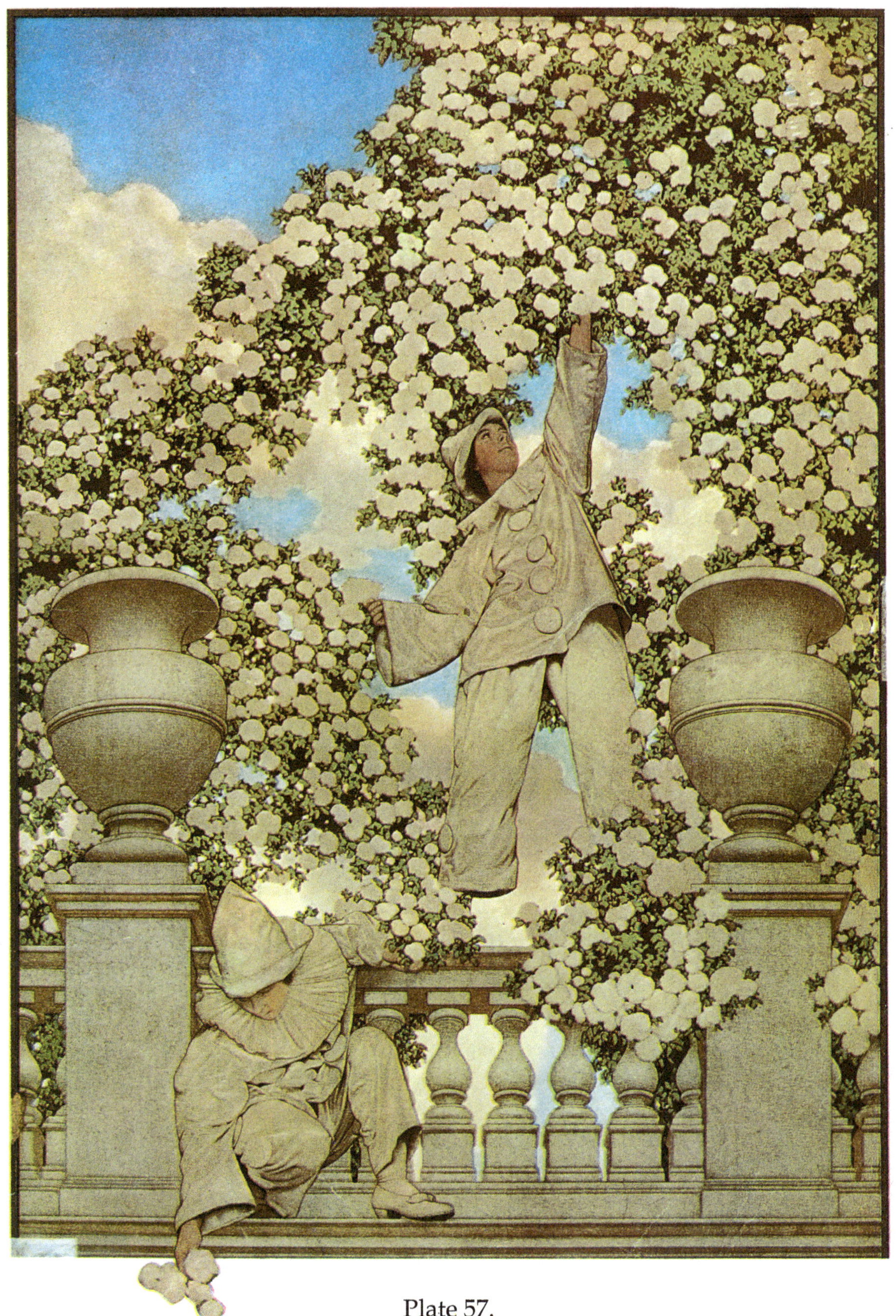

Plate 57.

Panel
The Curtis Publishing Company Mural, 1912–1915

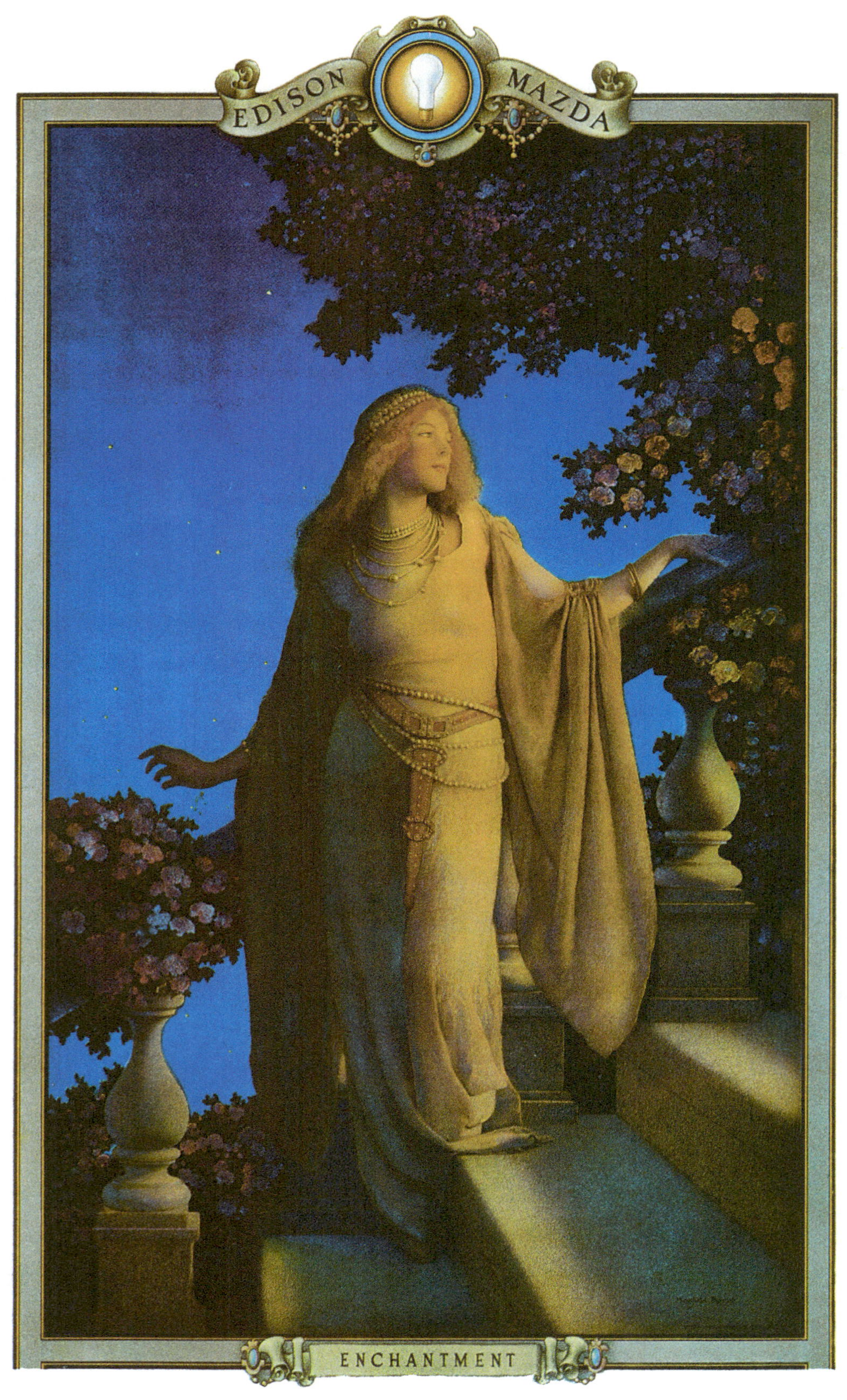

Plate 58.

Cinderella, aka *Enchantment* (painted in 1914)
Edison Mazda Lamps calendar, 1926

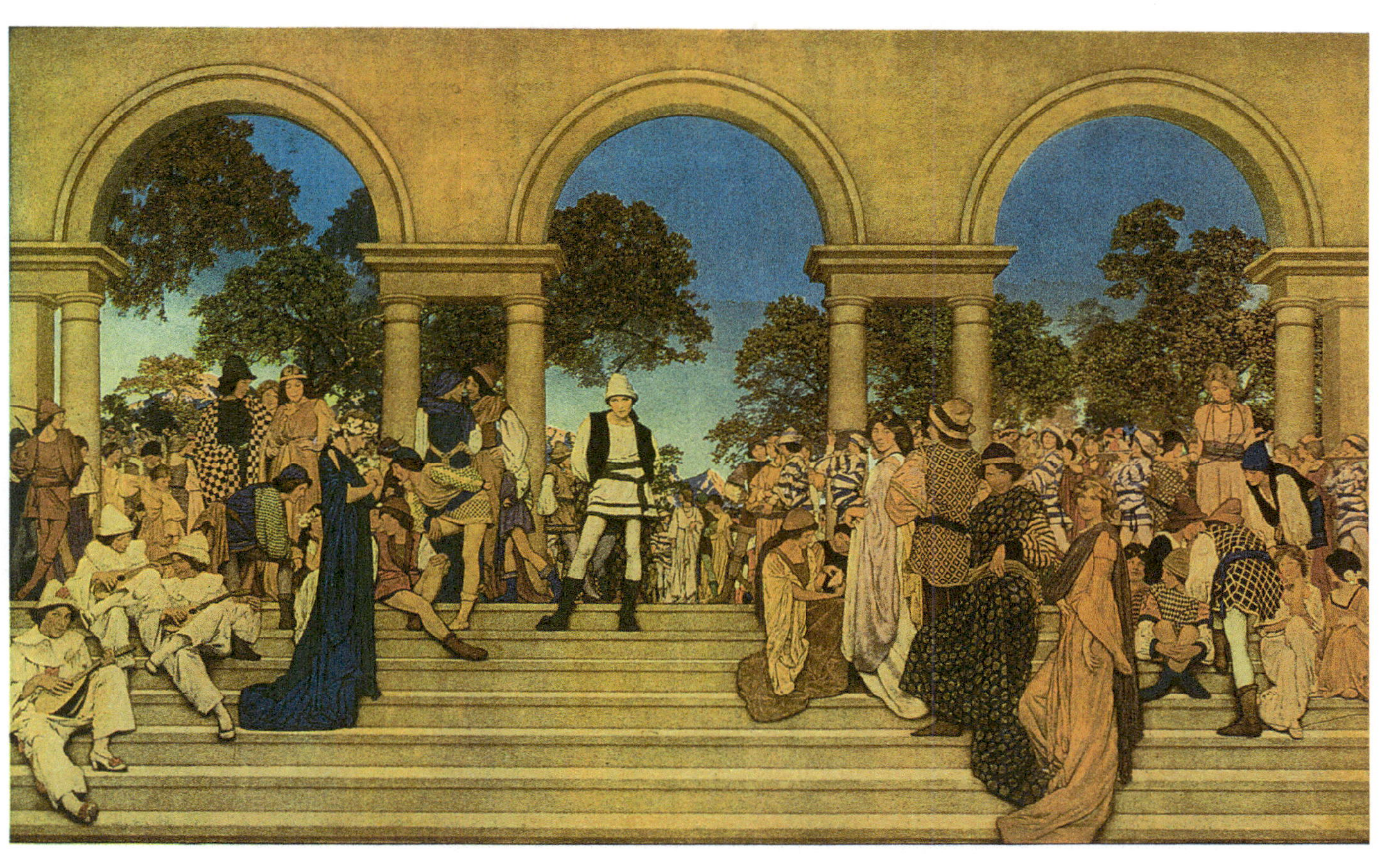

Plate 59.

Florentine Fête
Mural for Curtis Publishing, 1916

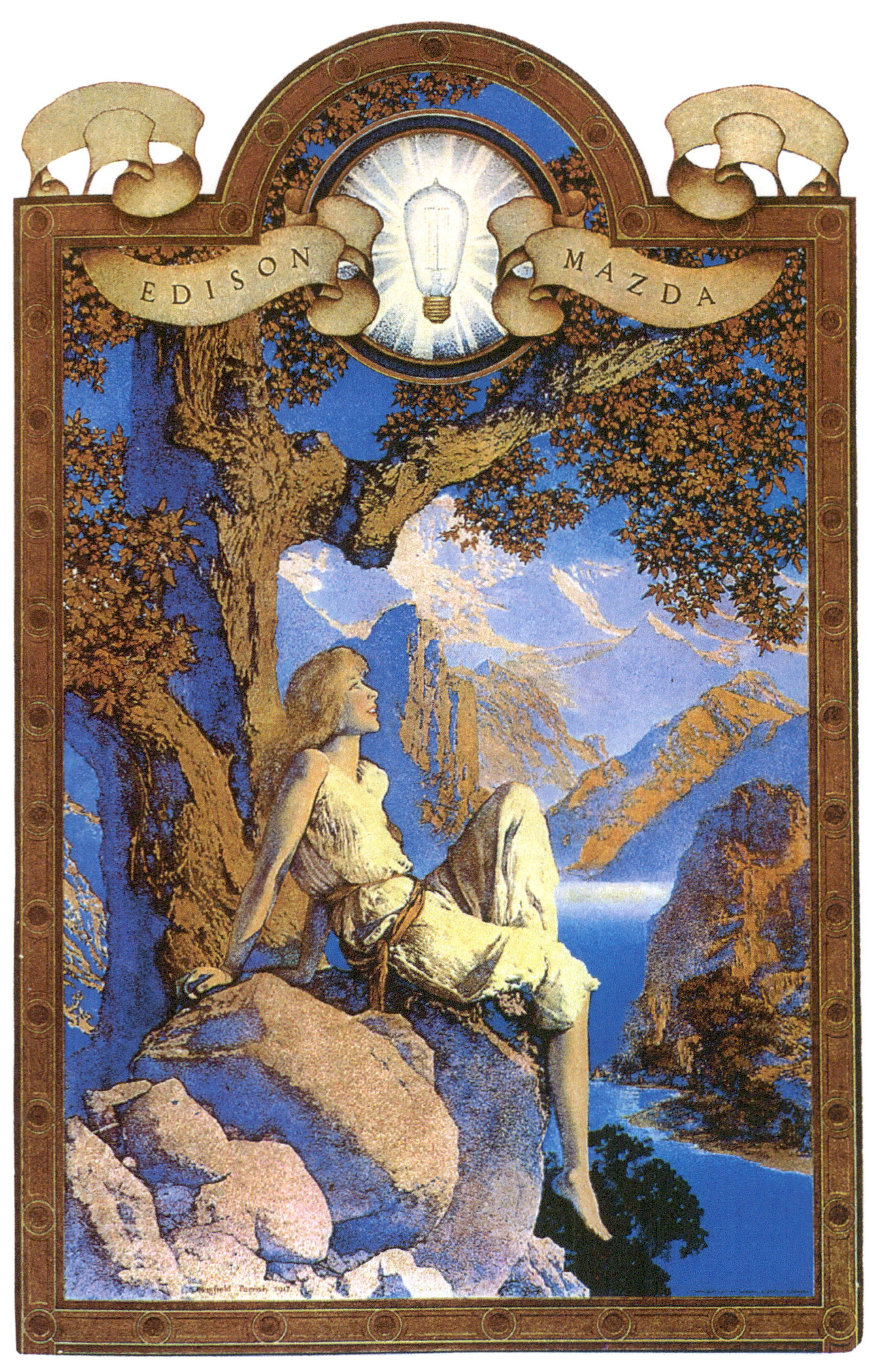

Plate 60.

And the Night Is Fled
Edison Mazda Lamps calendar, 1918

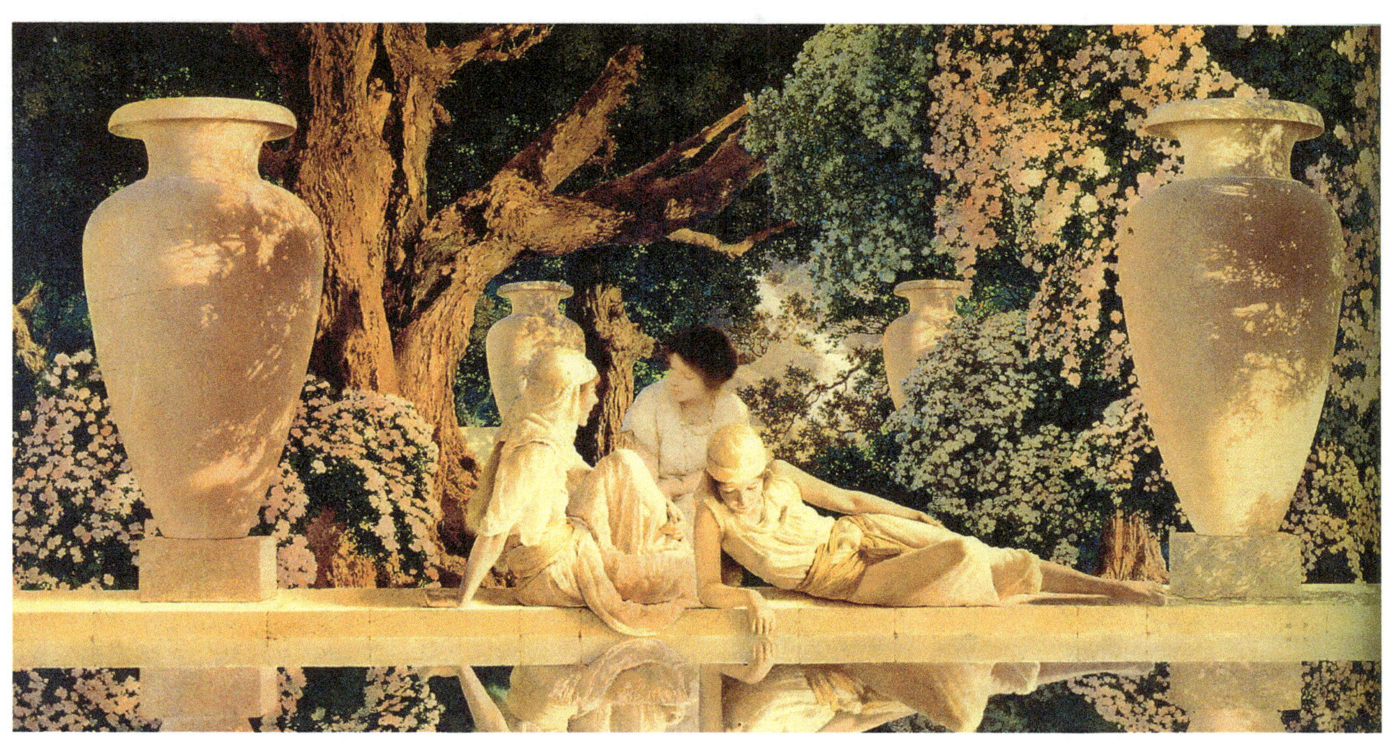

Plate 61.

Garden of Allah
Print, House of Art, 1918

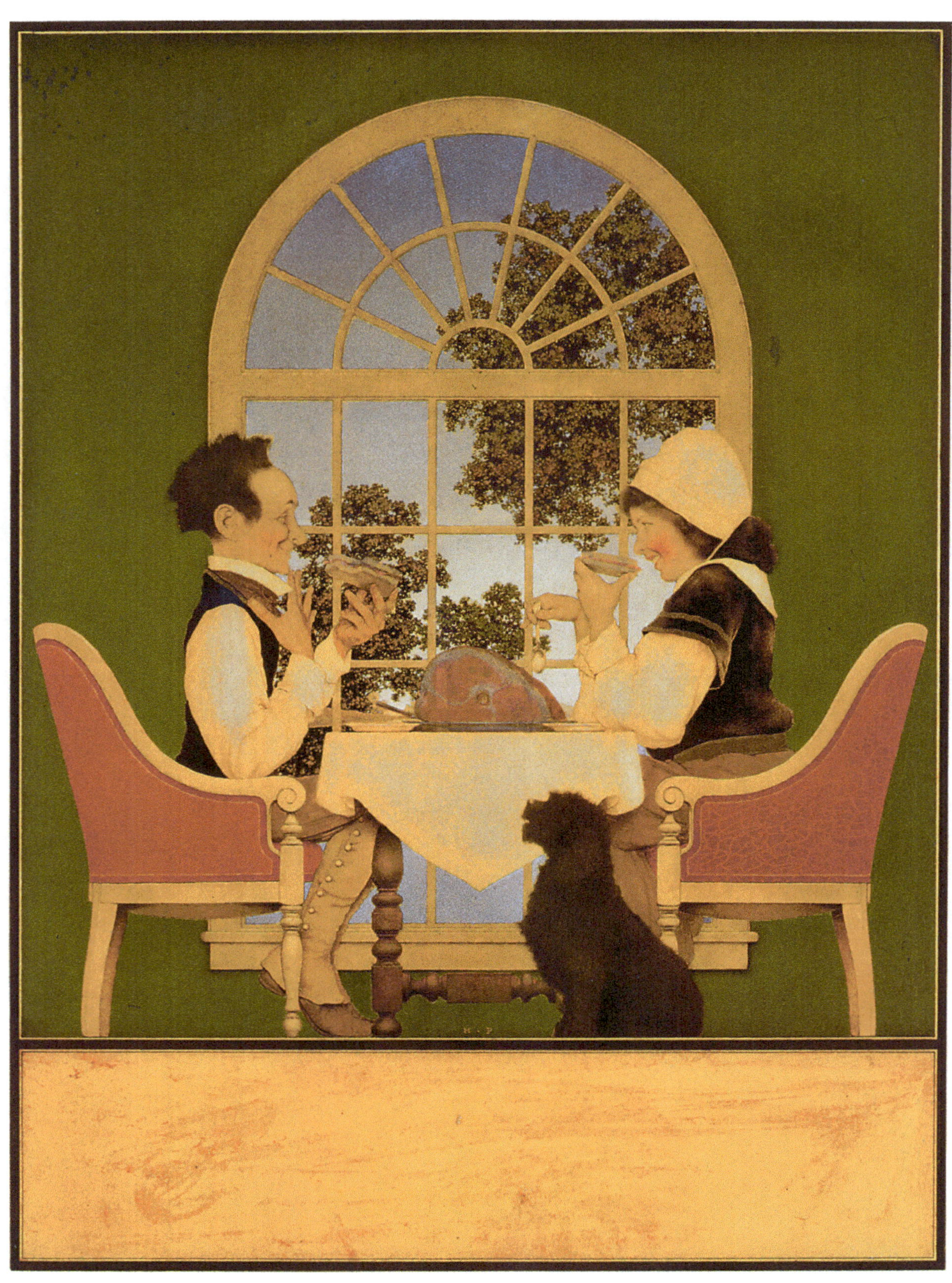

Plate 62.

Jack Sprat
Swift's Premium Ham Advertisement, 1919

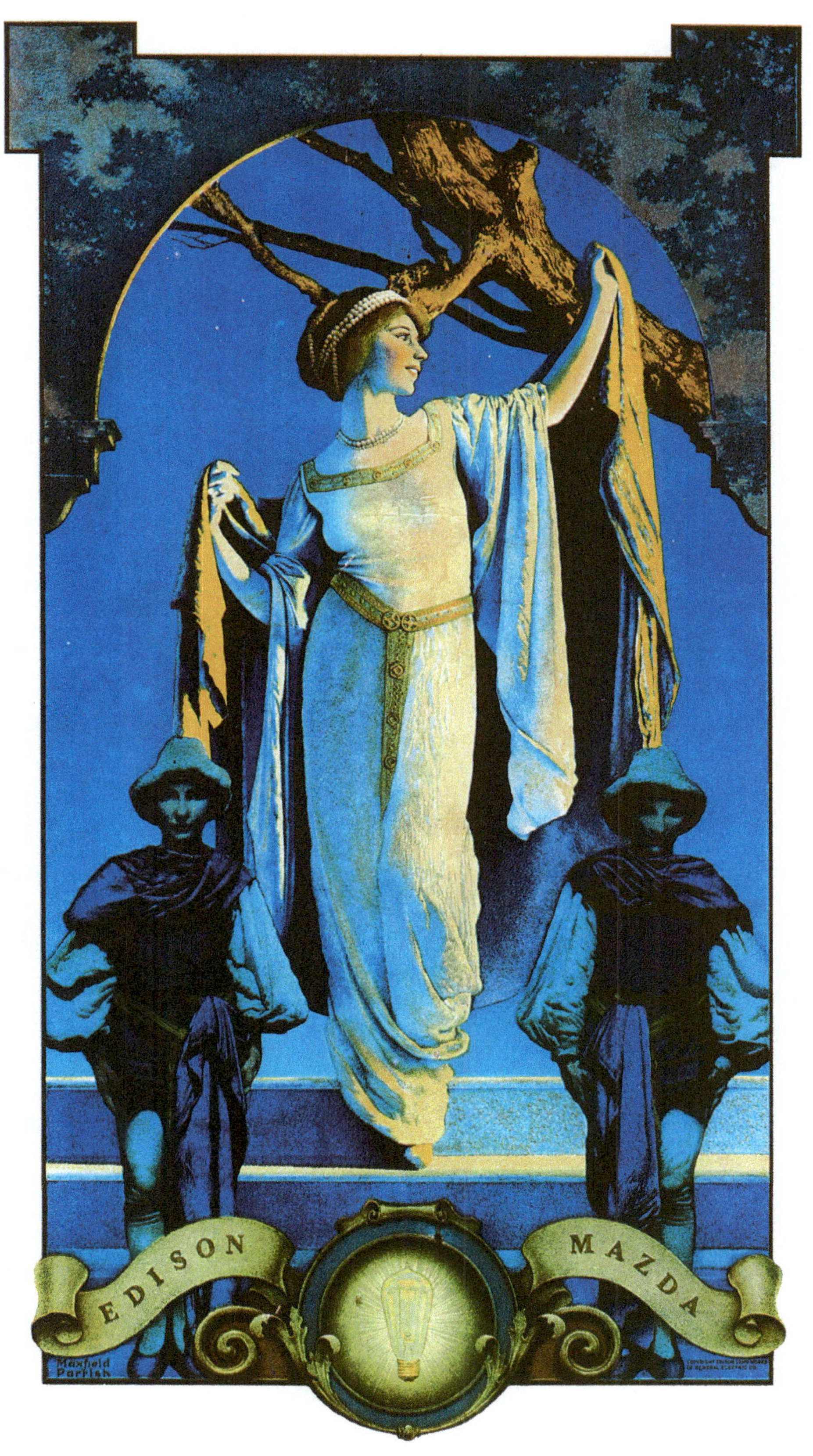

Plate 63.

Spirit of the Night
Edison Mazda Lamps calendar, 1919

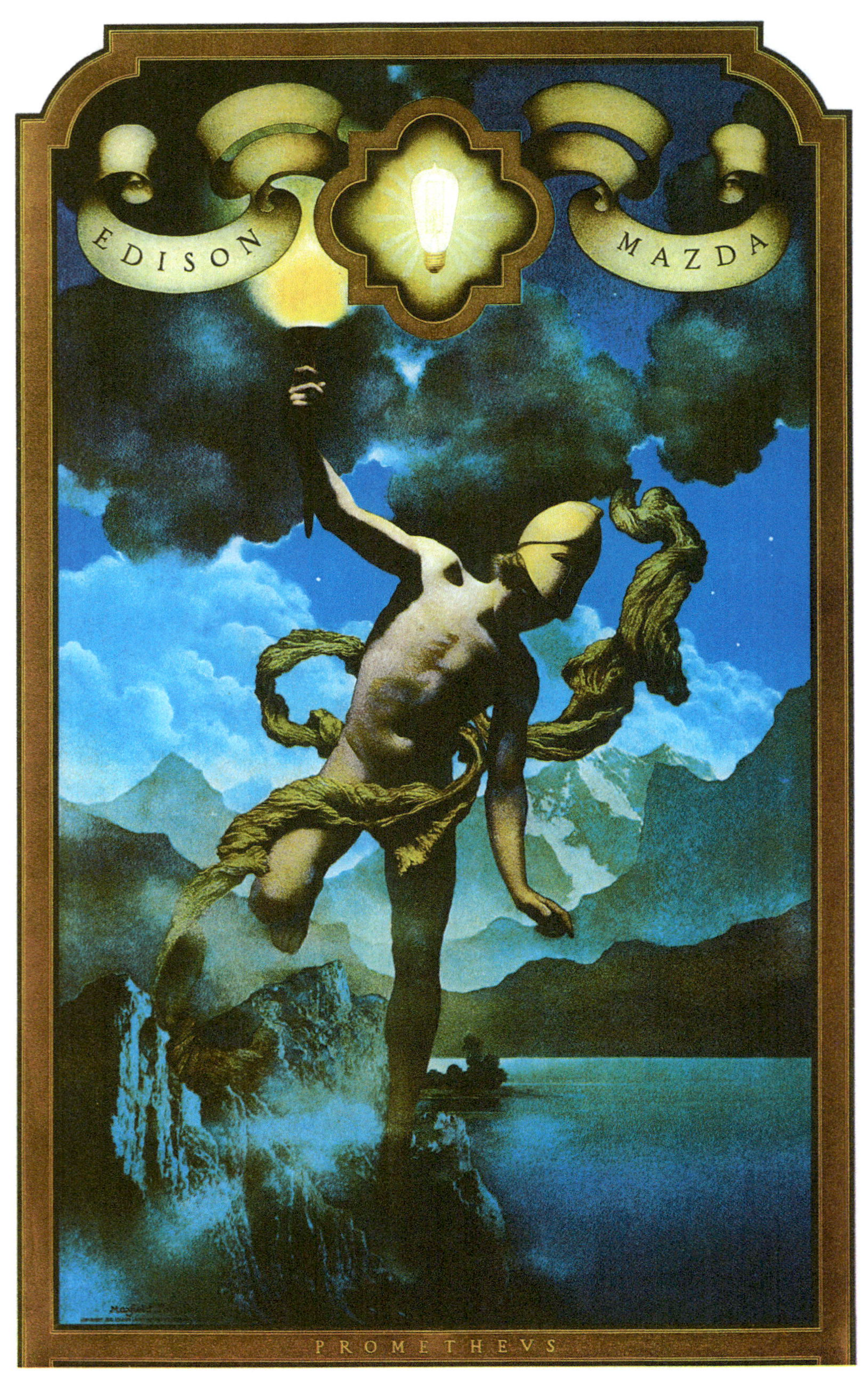

Plate 64.

Prometheus
Edison Mazda Lamps calendar, 1920

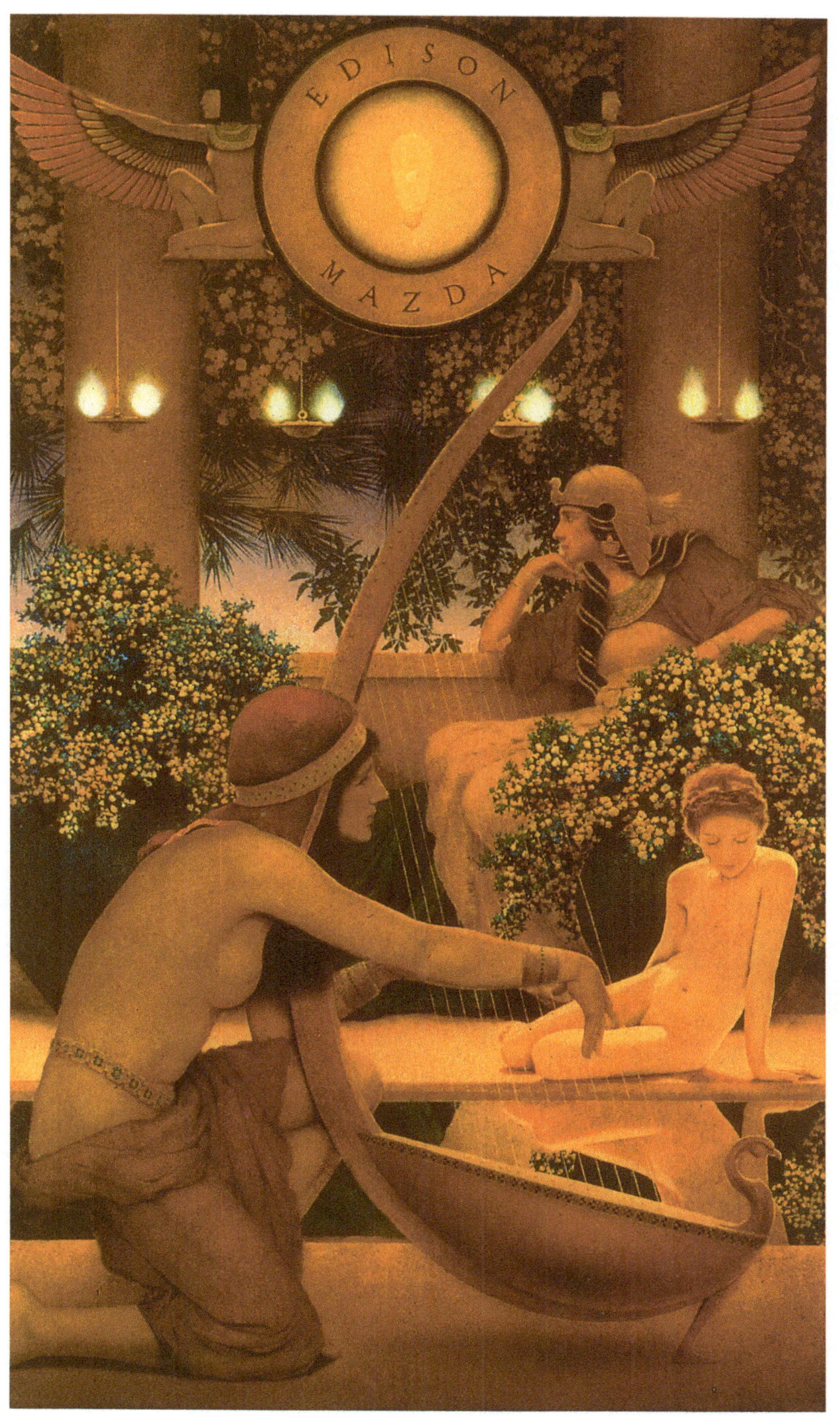

Plate 65.

Egypt
Edison Mazda Lamps calendar, 1922

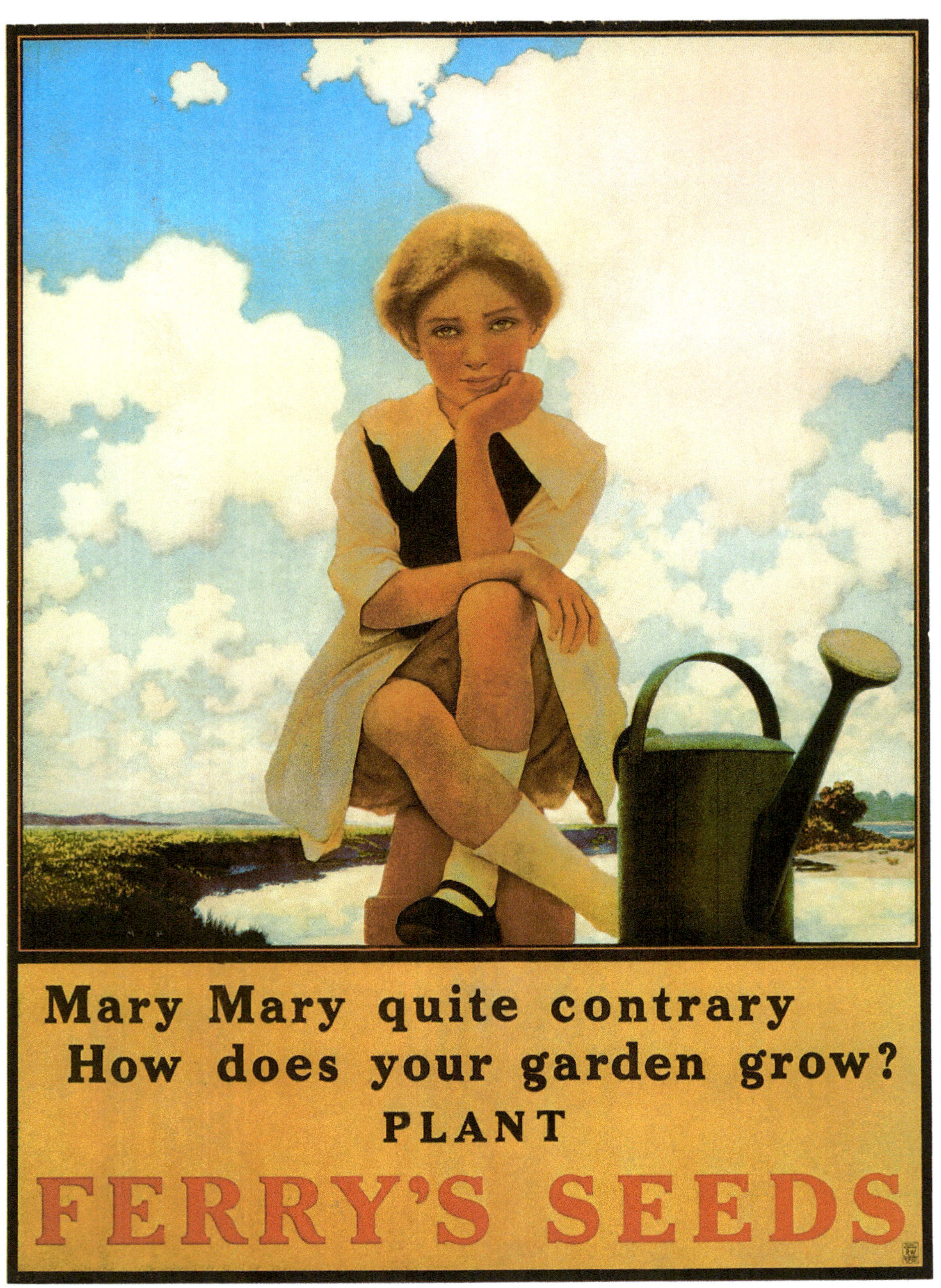

Plate 66.

Advertisement
Ferry's Seeds, 1921

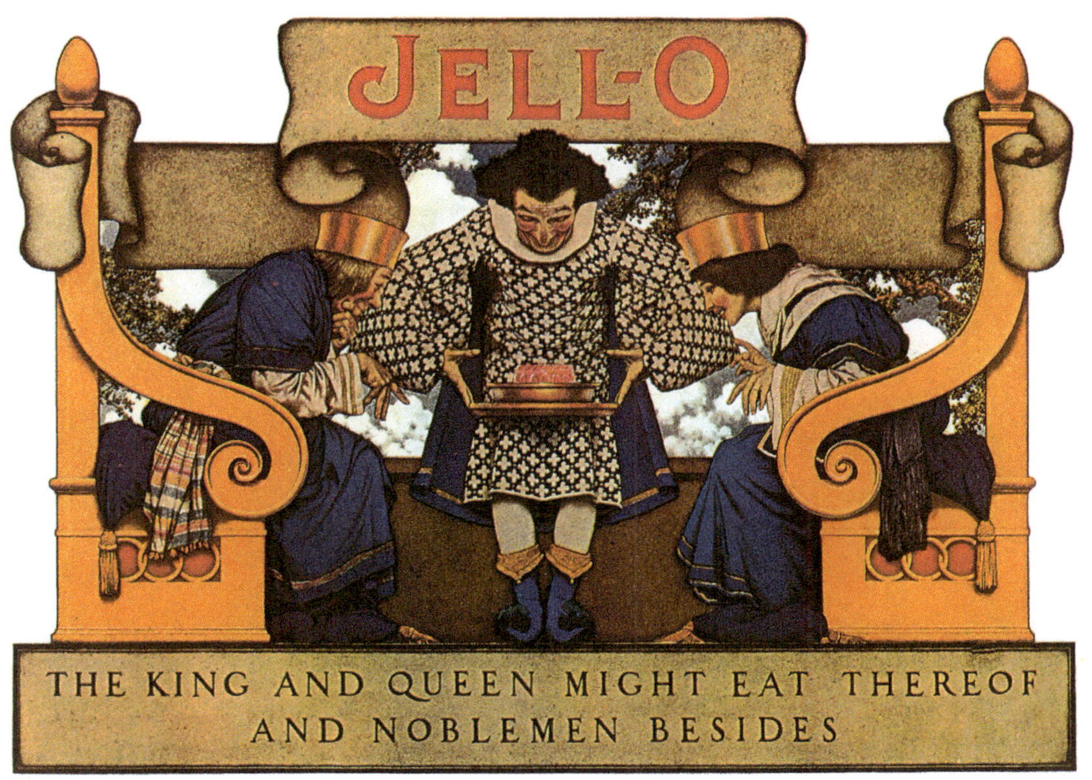

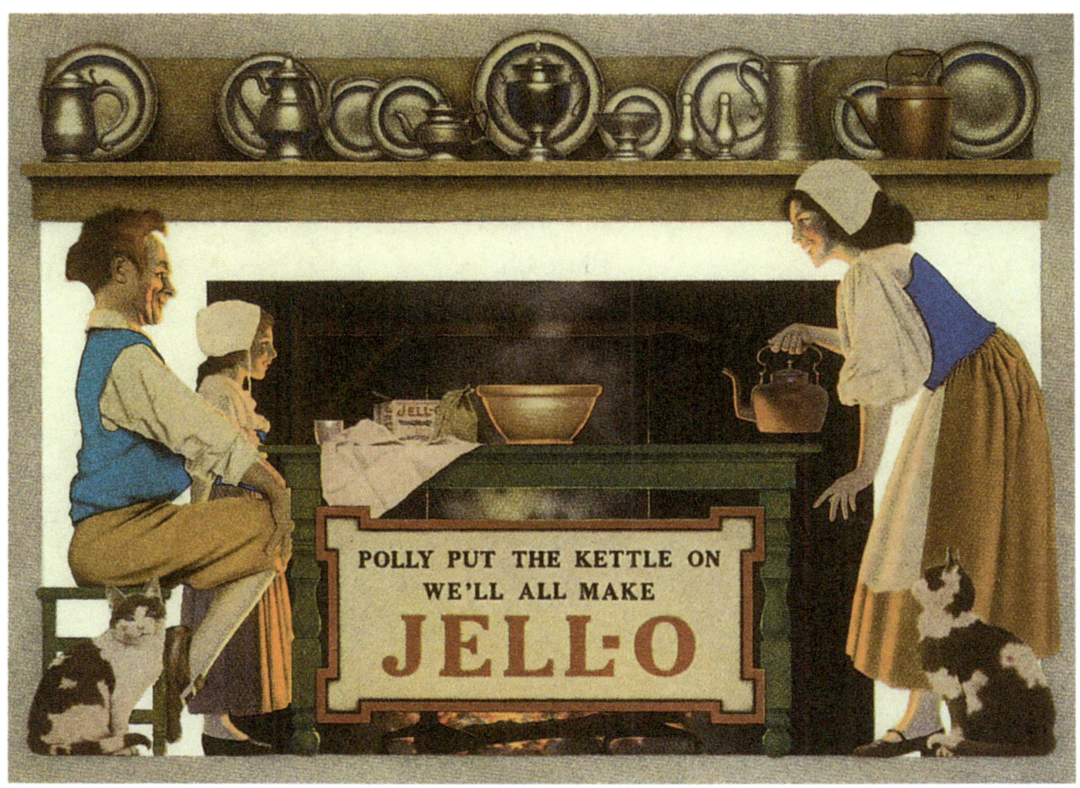

Plate 67.

King and Queen
Advertisement, Jell-O, 1921

Polly put the Kettle on
Advertisement, Jell-O, 1921

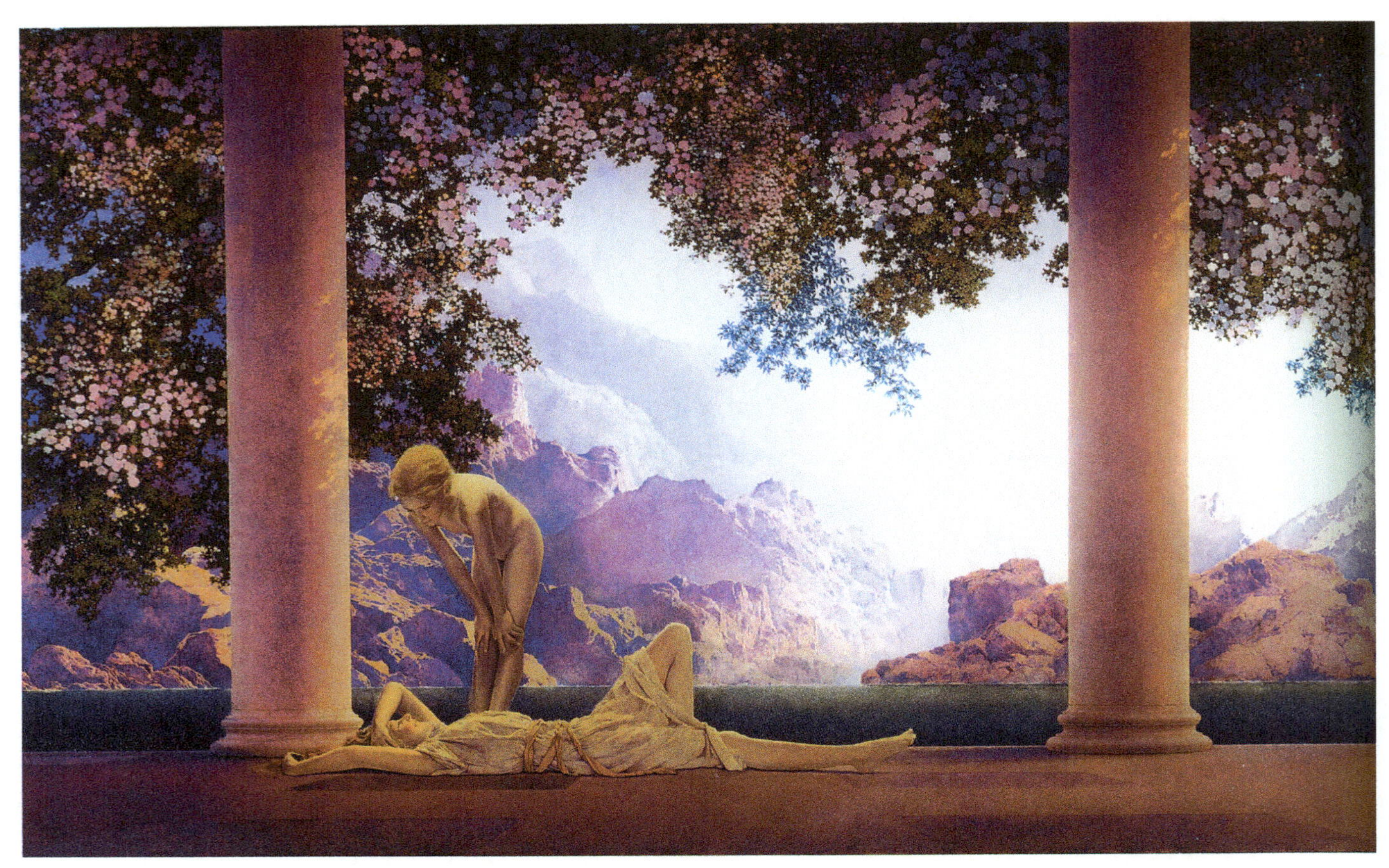

Plate 68.

Daybreak
Print, House of Art, 1922

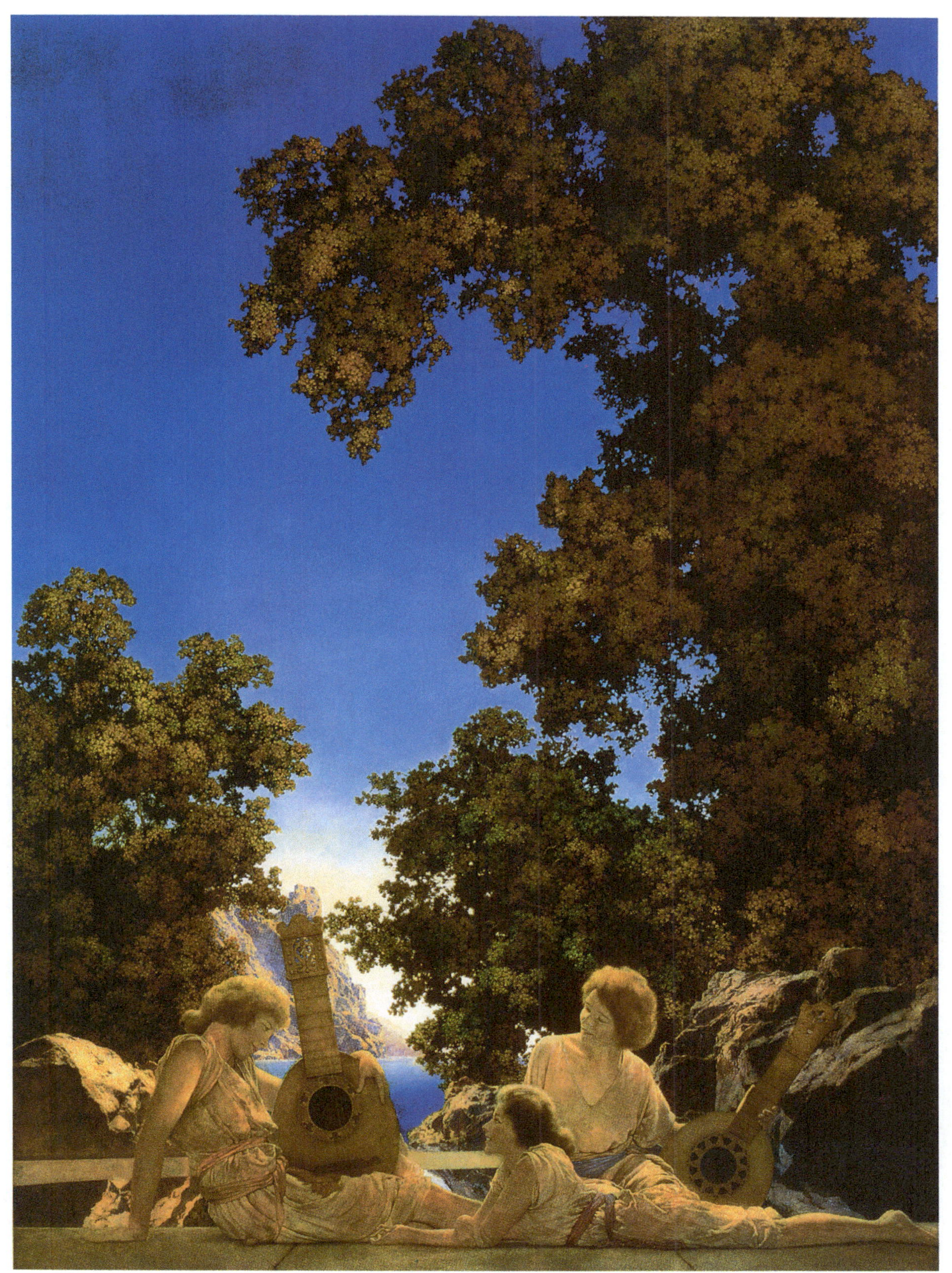

Plate 69.

Interlude

Mural

The Memorial Art Gallery of the University of Rochester, 1922

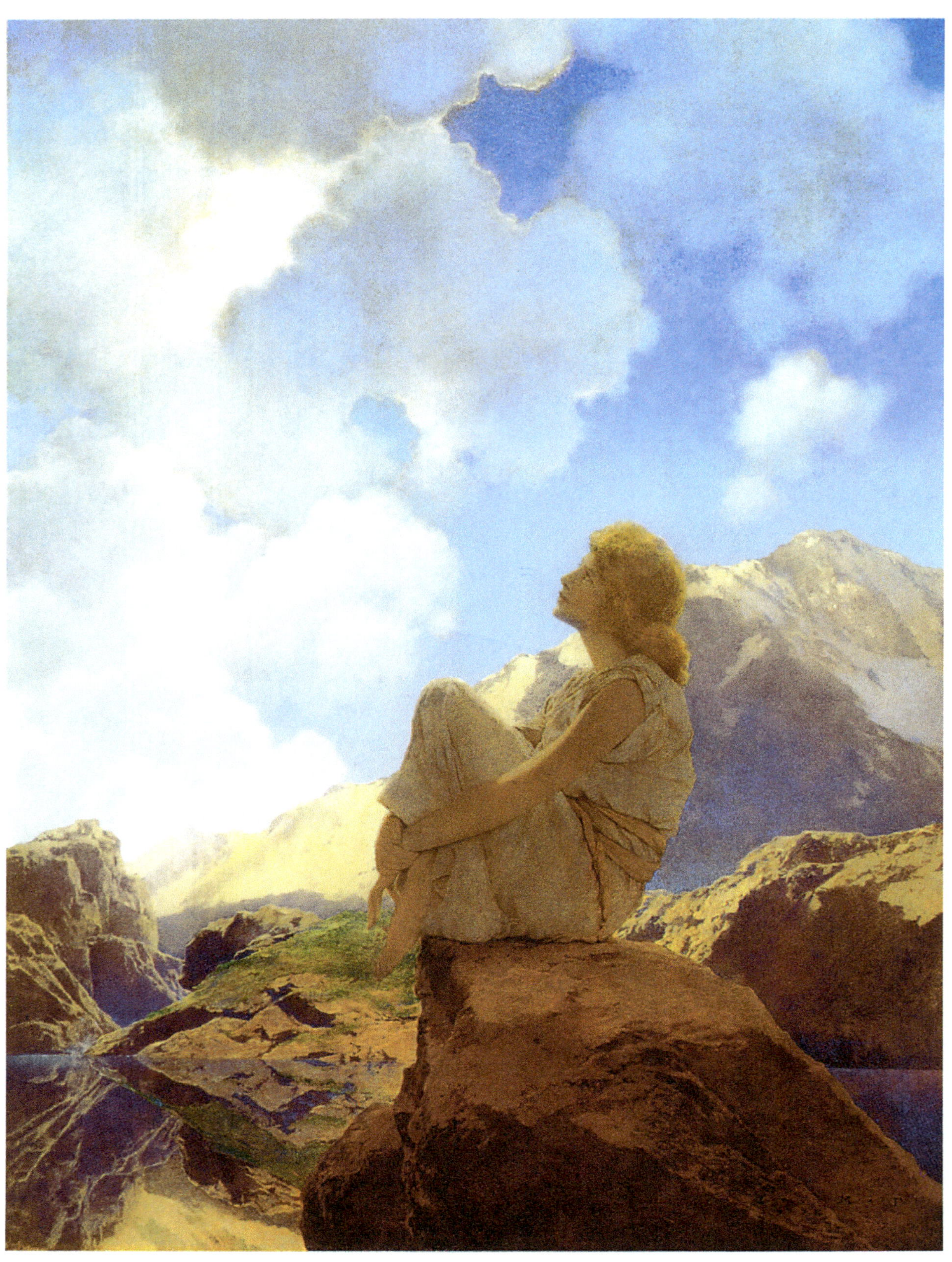

Plate 70.

Morning

Cover, *Life* magazine, April 1922

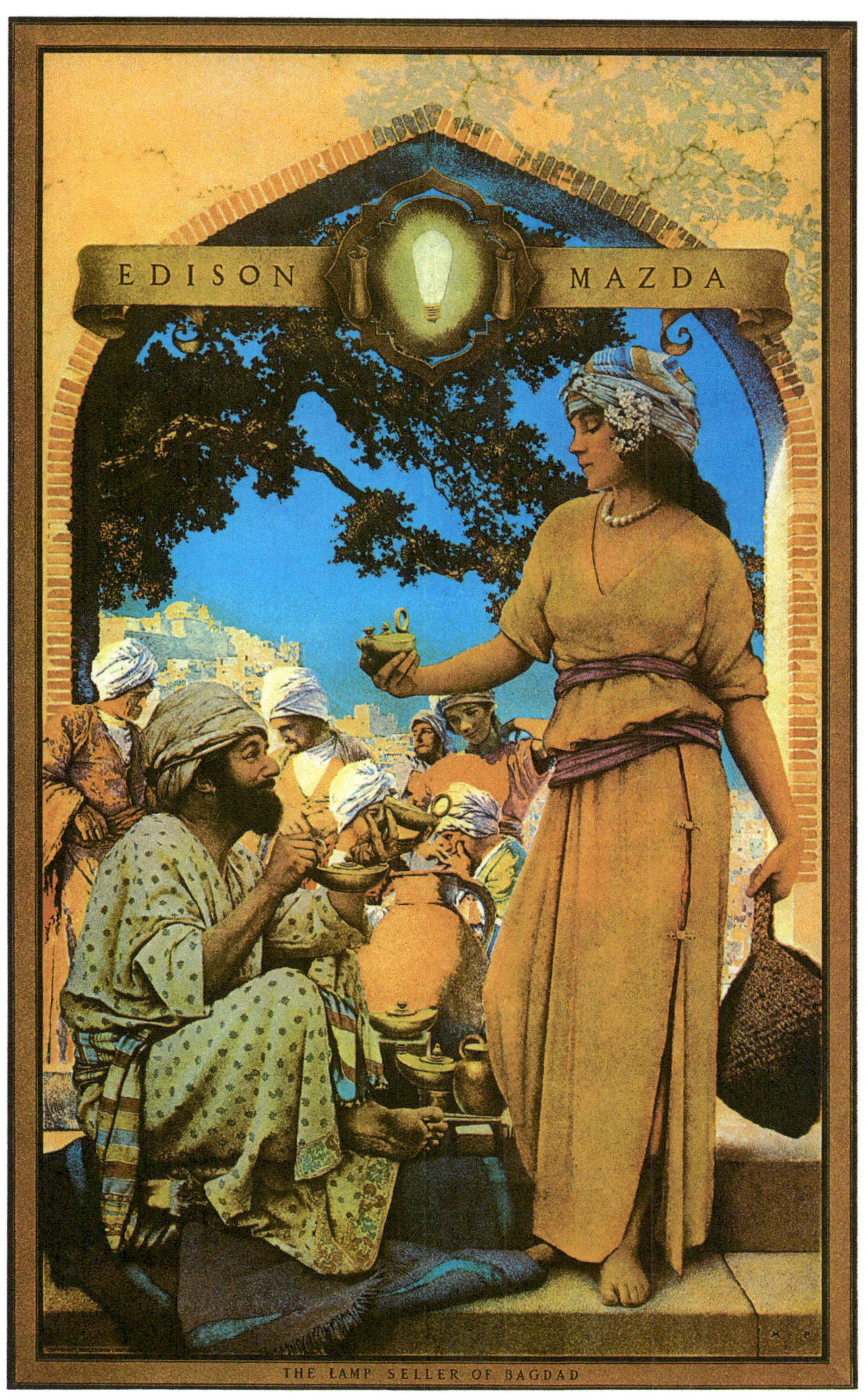

Plate 71.

The Lamp Seller of Bag[h]dad
Edison Mazda Lamps calendar, 1923

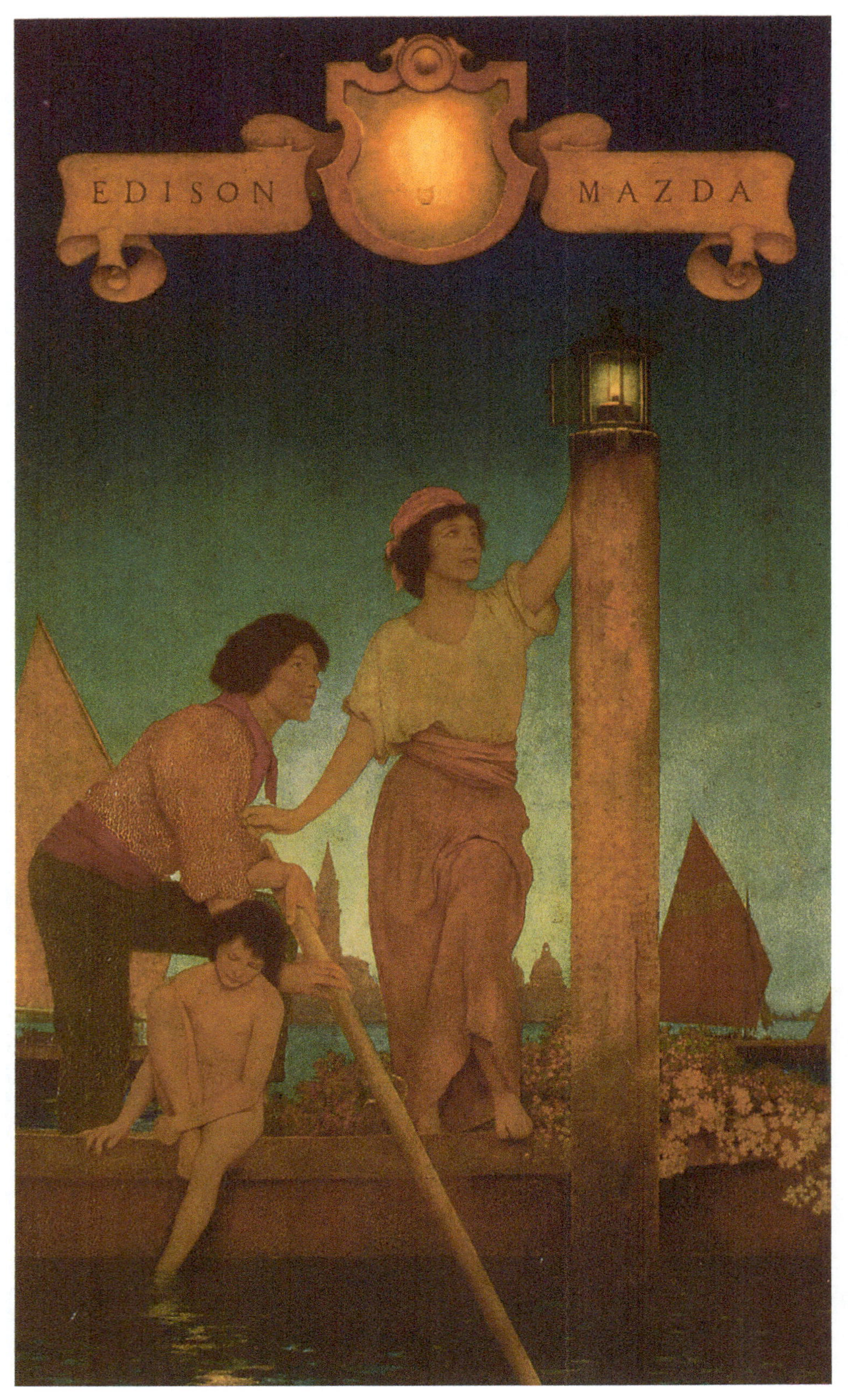

Plate 72.

Venetian Lamplighter
Edison Mazda Lamps calendar, 1924

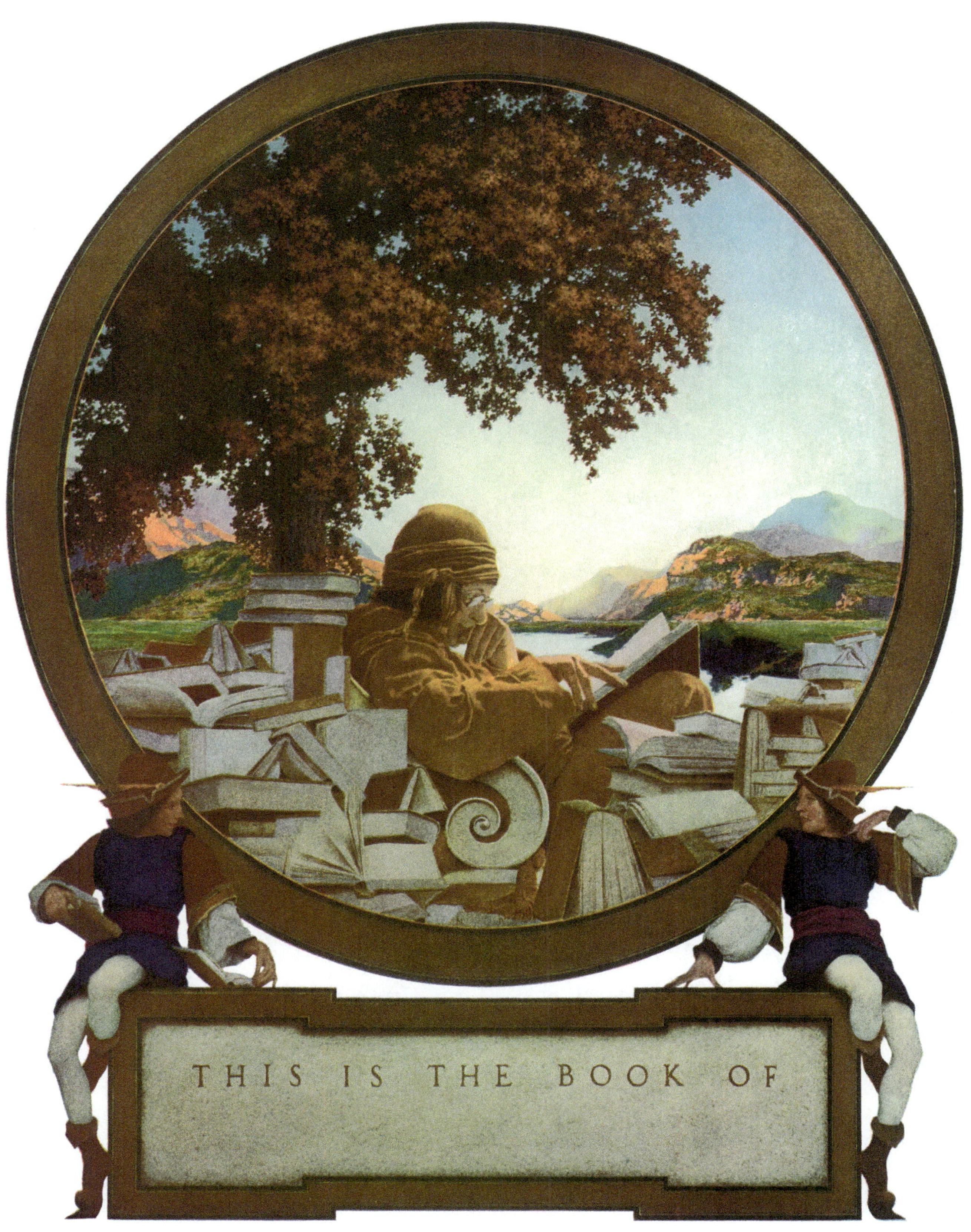

Plate 73.

Bookplate: This Is the Book of
The Knave of Hearts, 1925

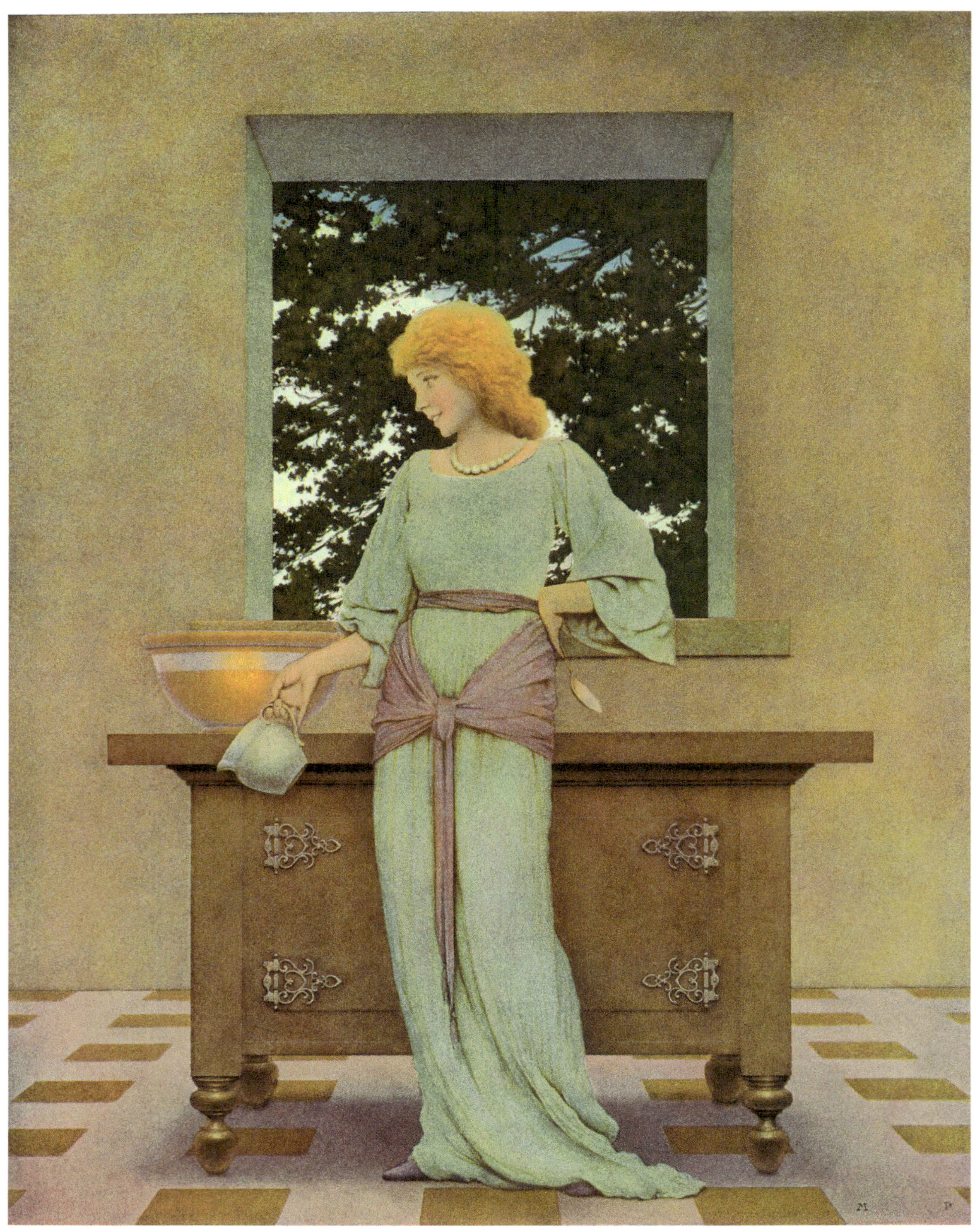

Plate 74.

Frontispiece: Lady Violetta
The Knave of Hearts, 1925

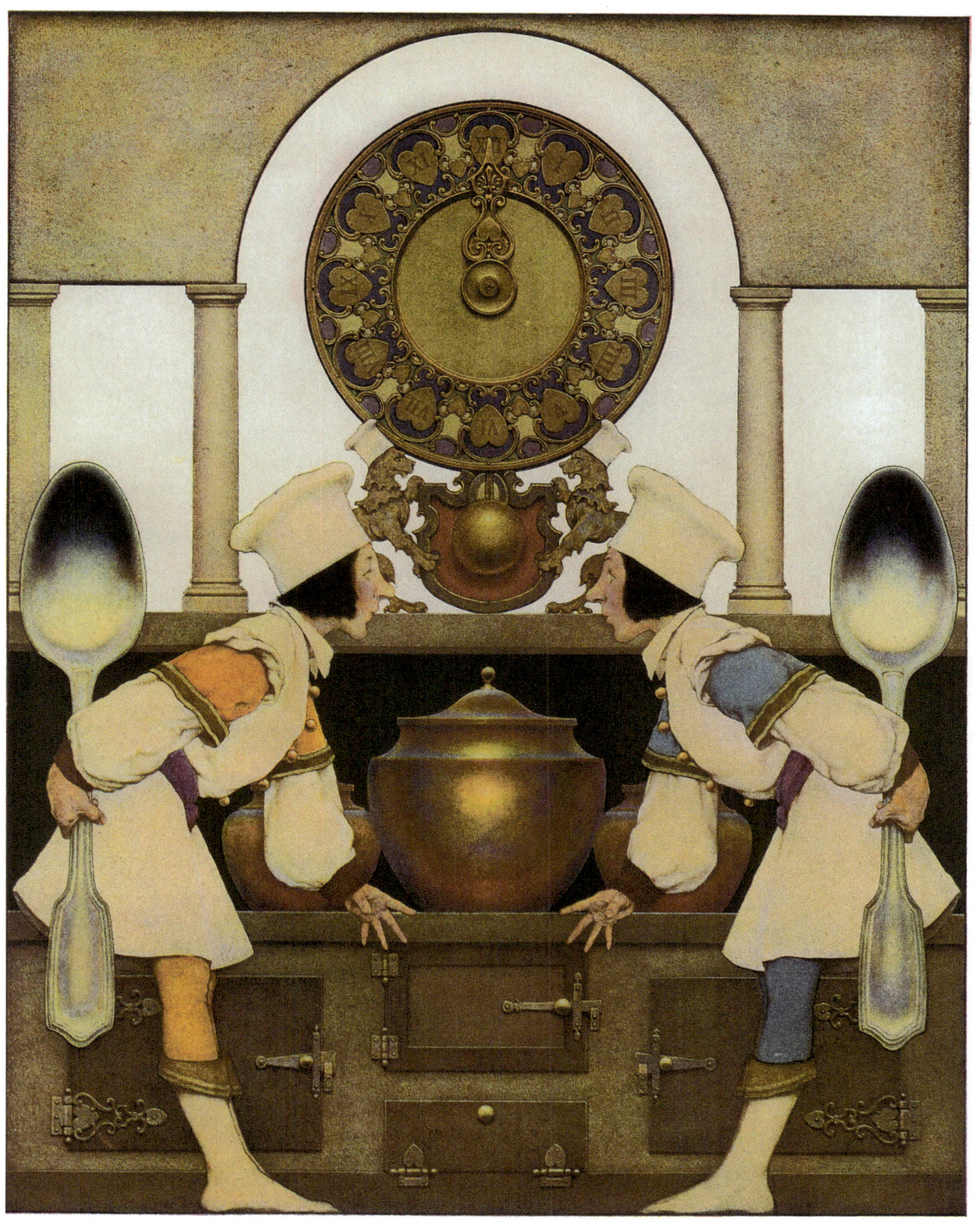

Plate 75.

Blue Hose/Yellow Hose
The Knave of Hearts, 1925

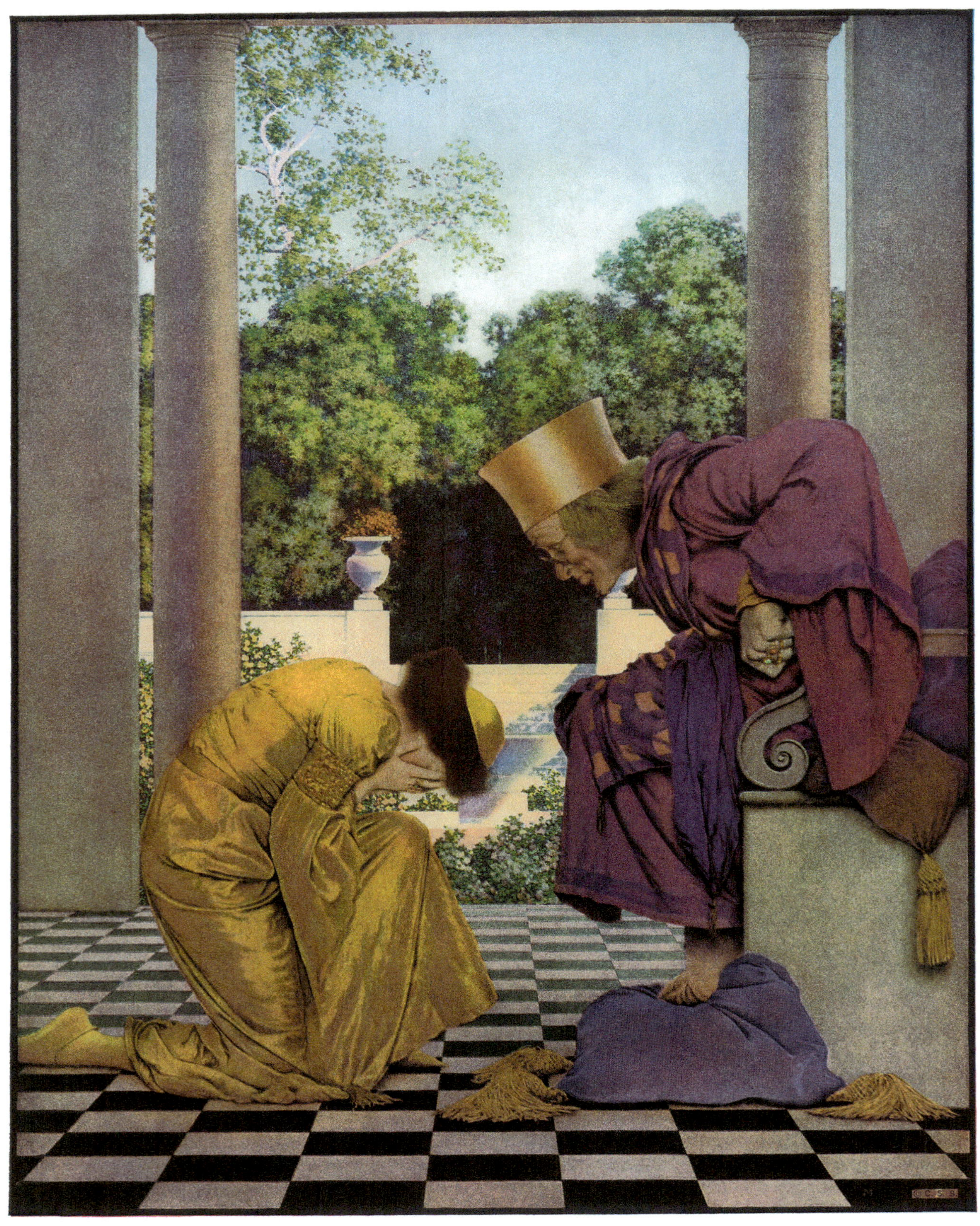

Plate 76.

Lady Ursula kneeling before the King
The Knave of Hearts, 1925

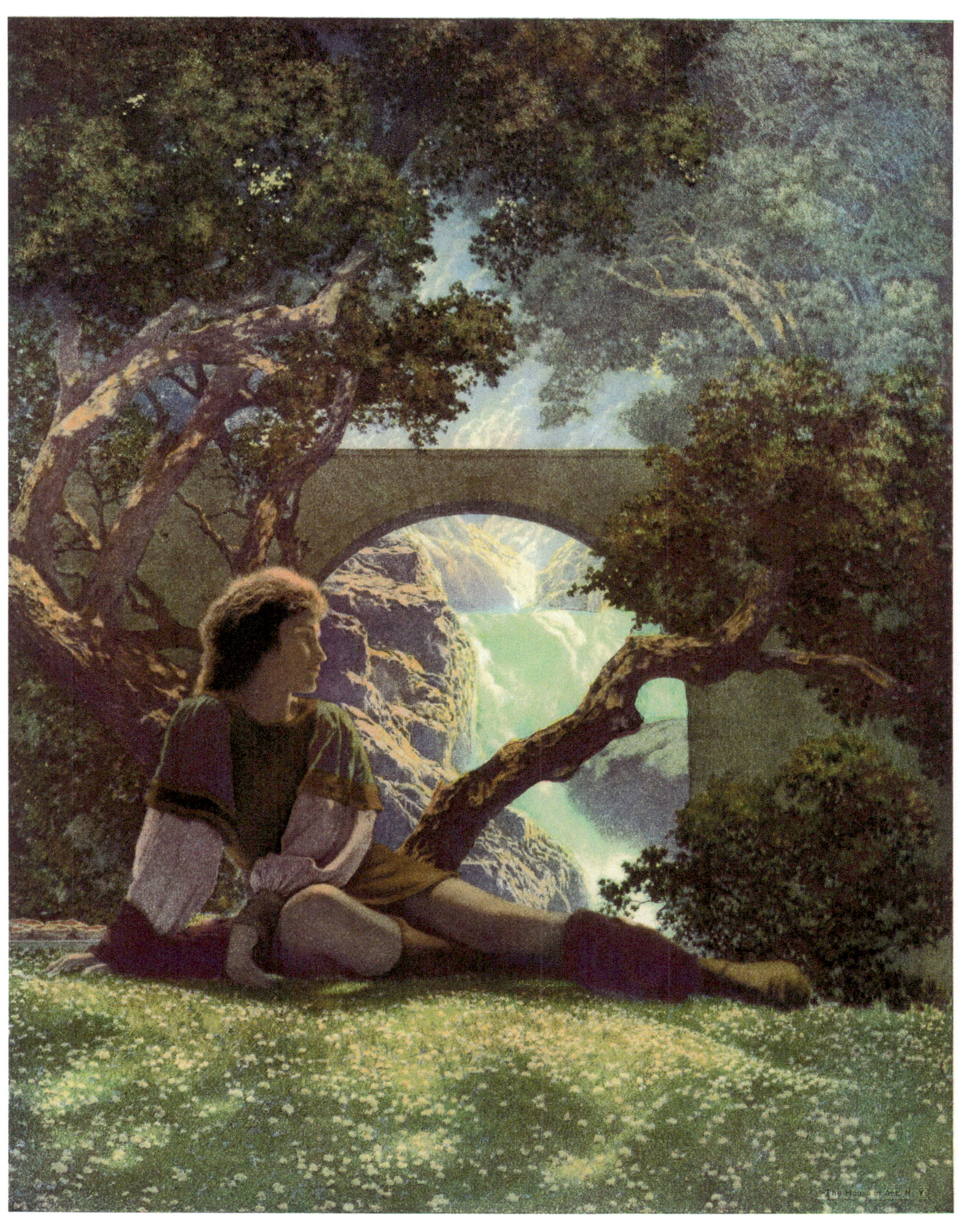

Plate 77.

The Knave

The Knave of Hearts, 1925

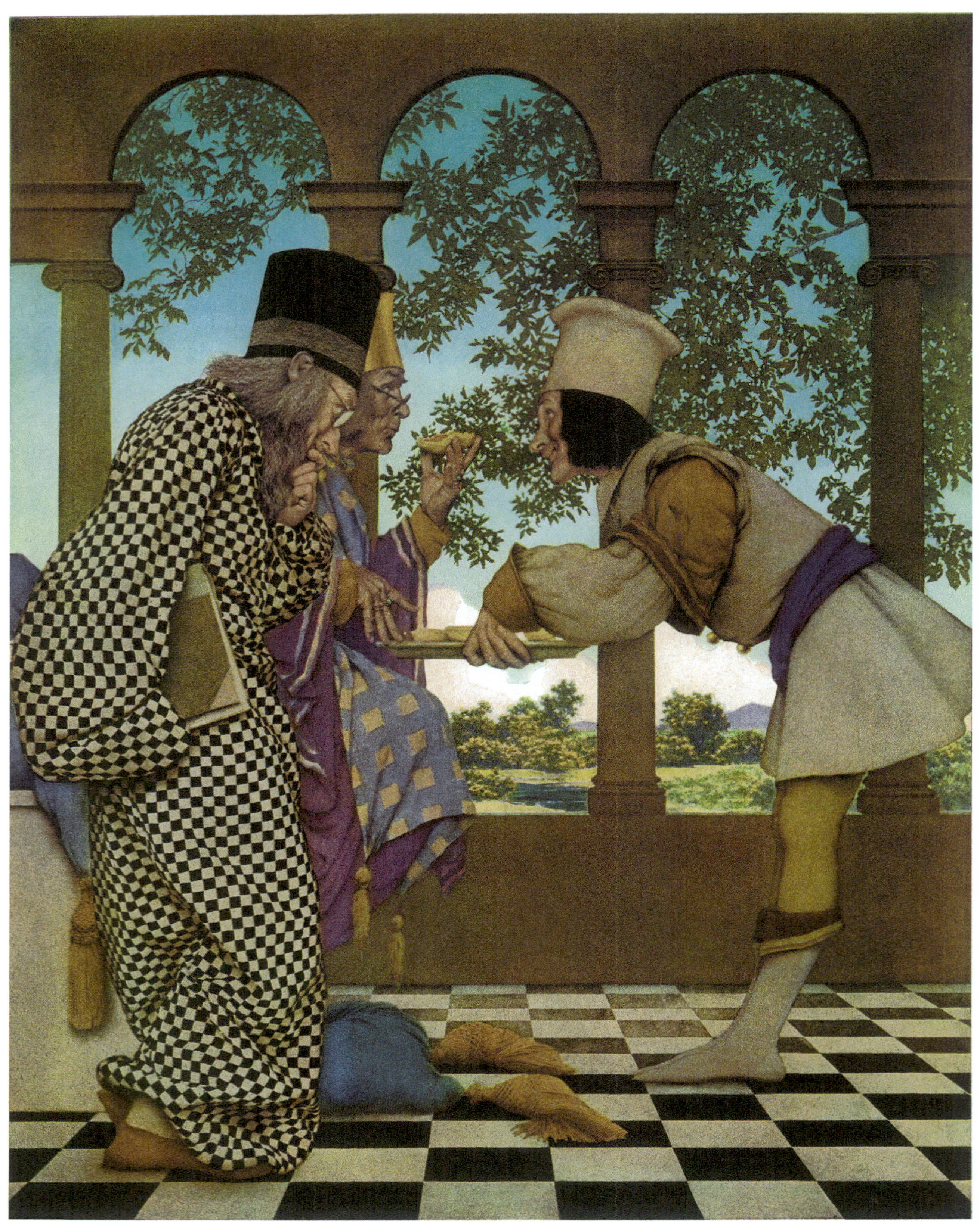

Plate 78.

The Chancellor, the King, and Yellow Hose
The Knave of Hearts, 1925

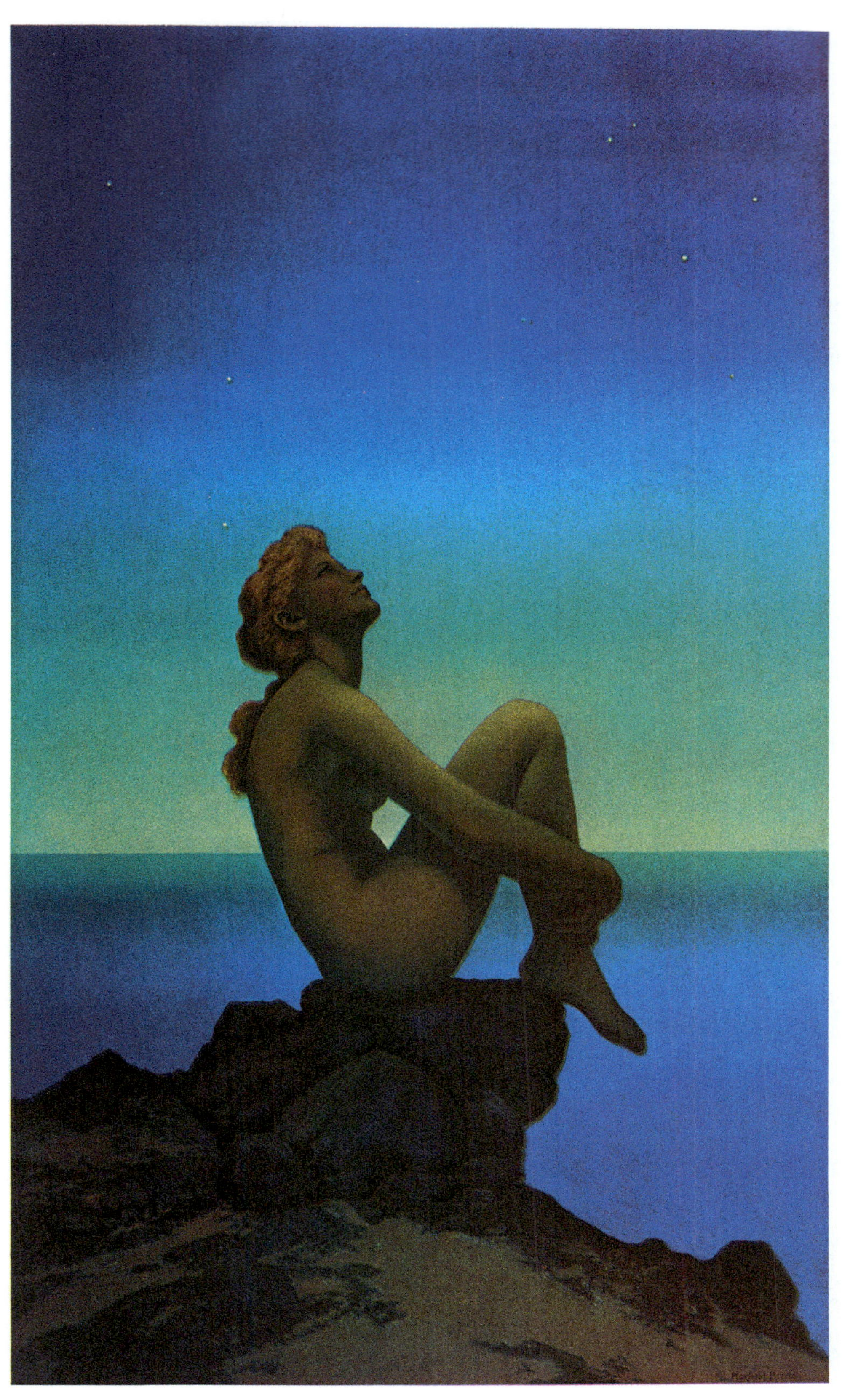

Plate 79.

Stars

Print, House of Art, 1926

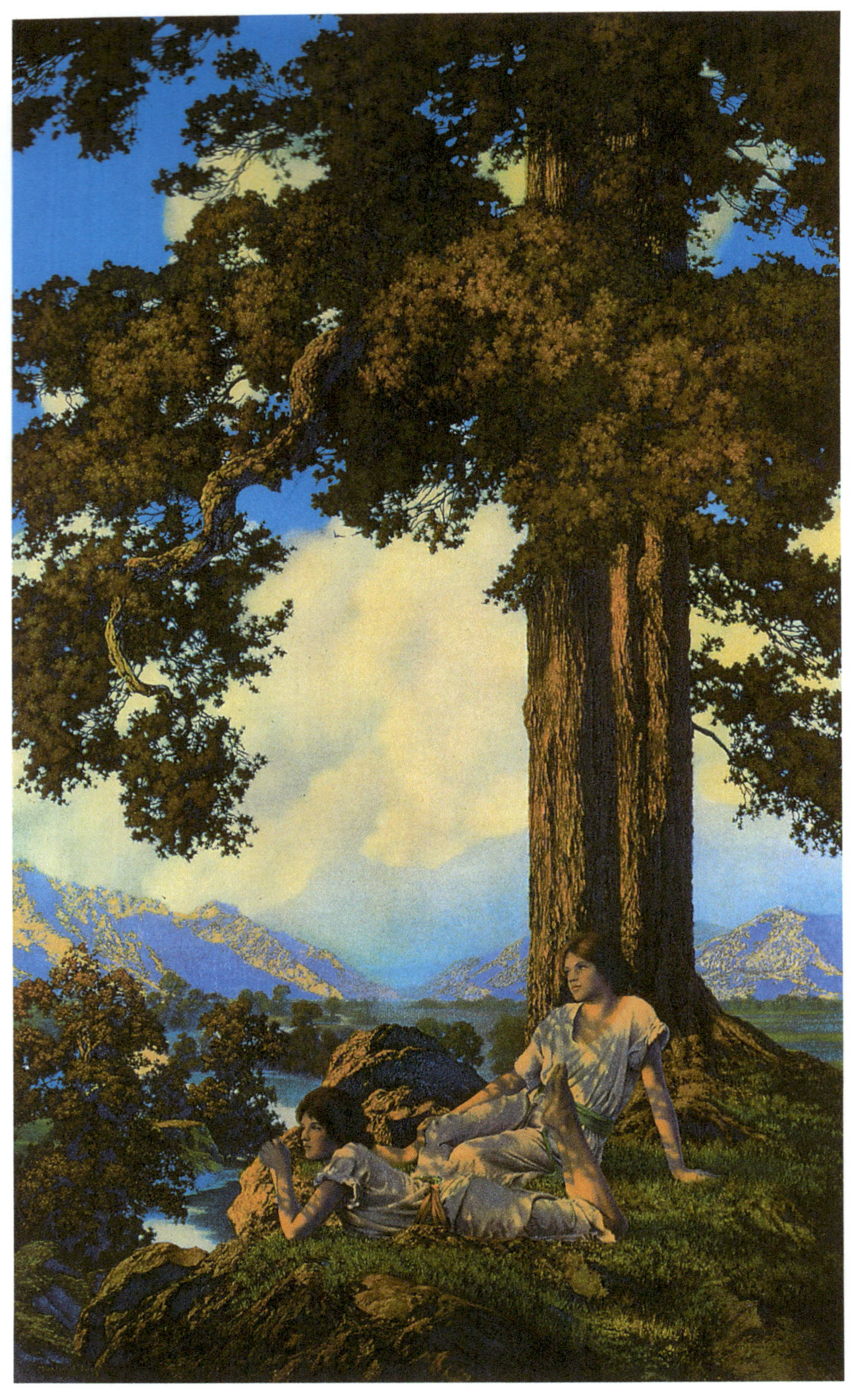

Plate 80

Hilltop
Print, House of Art, 1926

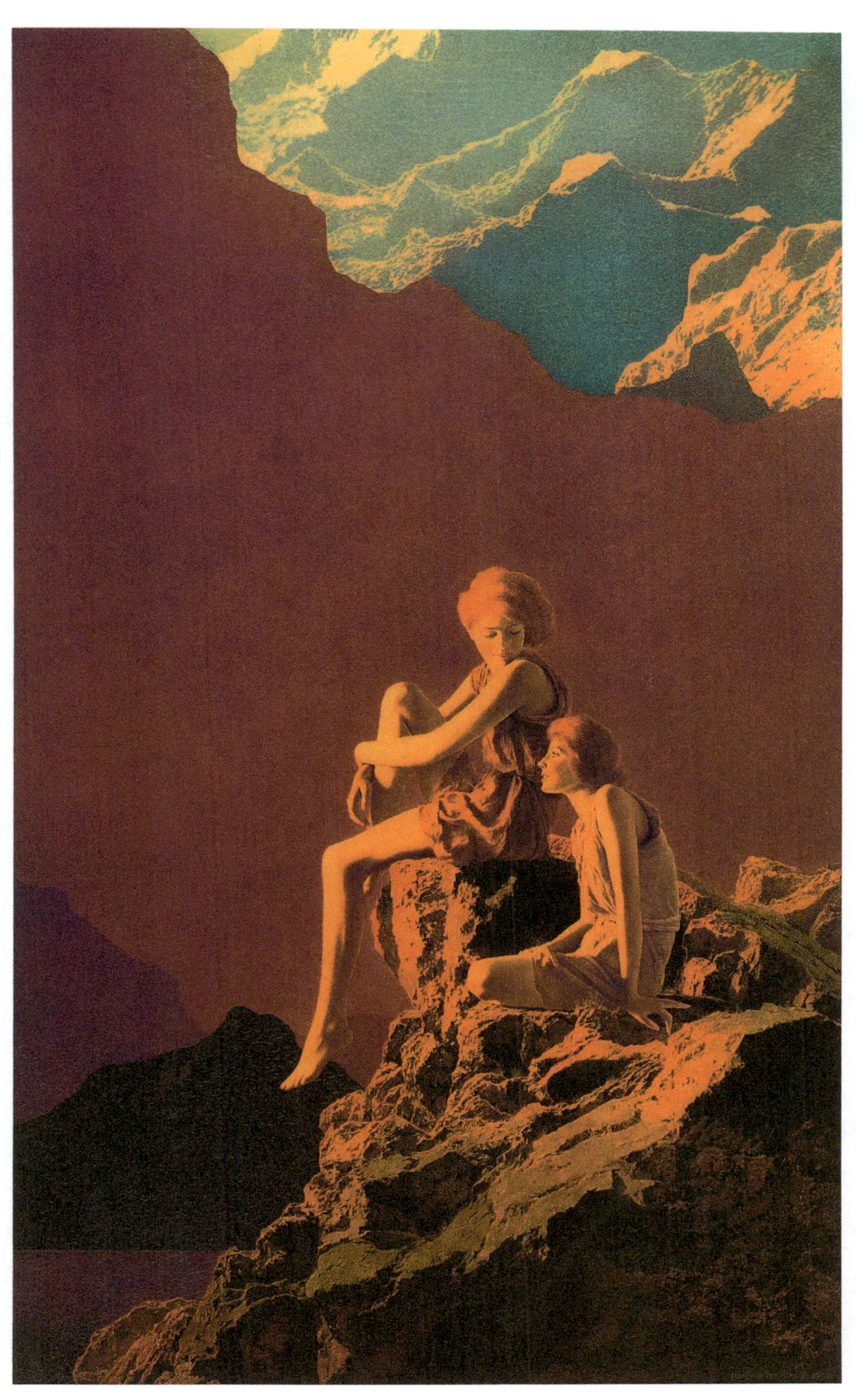

Plate 81.

Contentment

Edison Mazda Lamps calendar, 1928

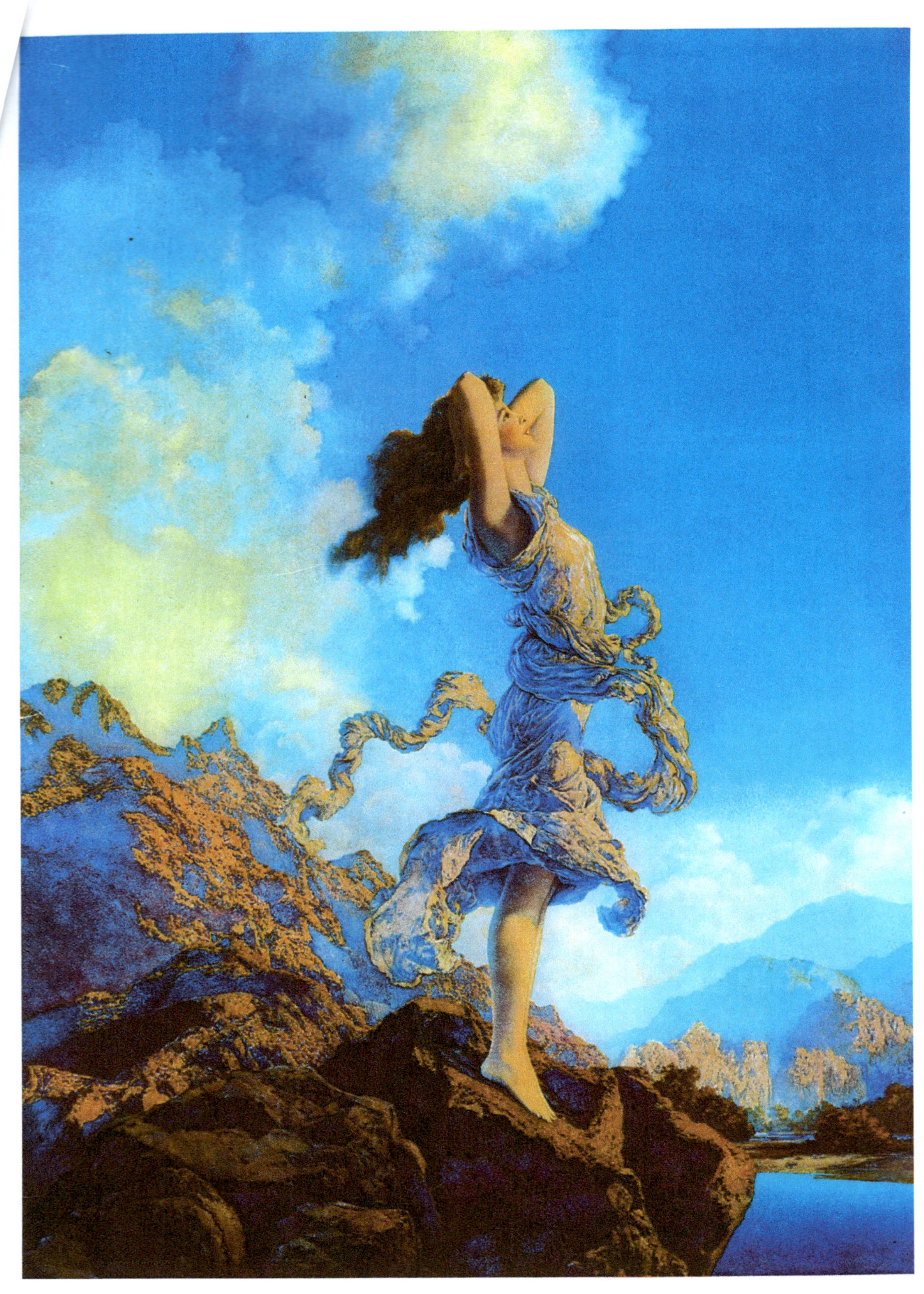

Plate 82.

Ecstasy

Edison Mazda Lamps calendar, 1930

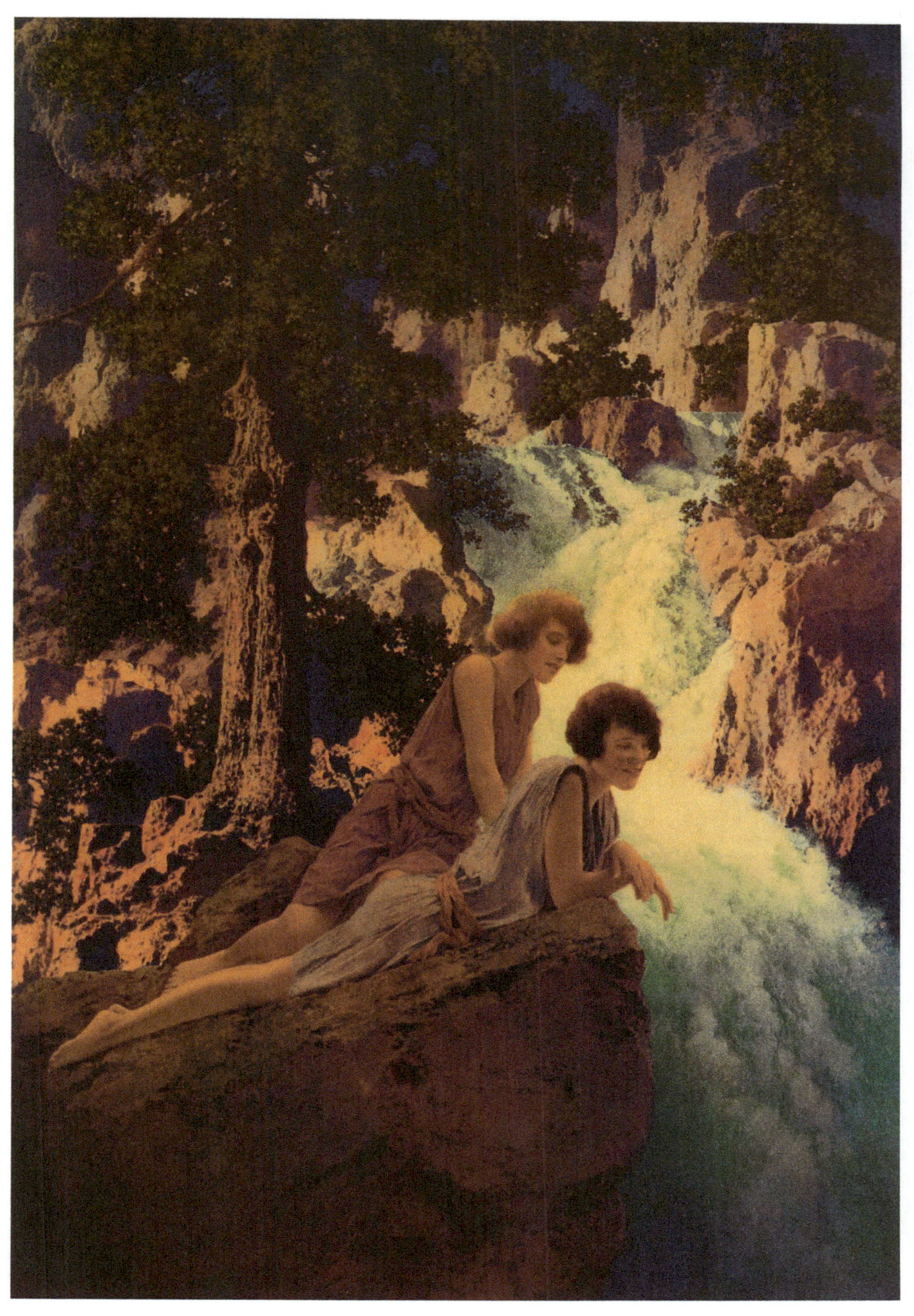

Plate 83.

Waterfall

Edison Mazda Lamps calendar, 1931

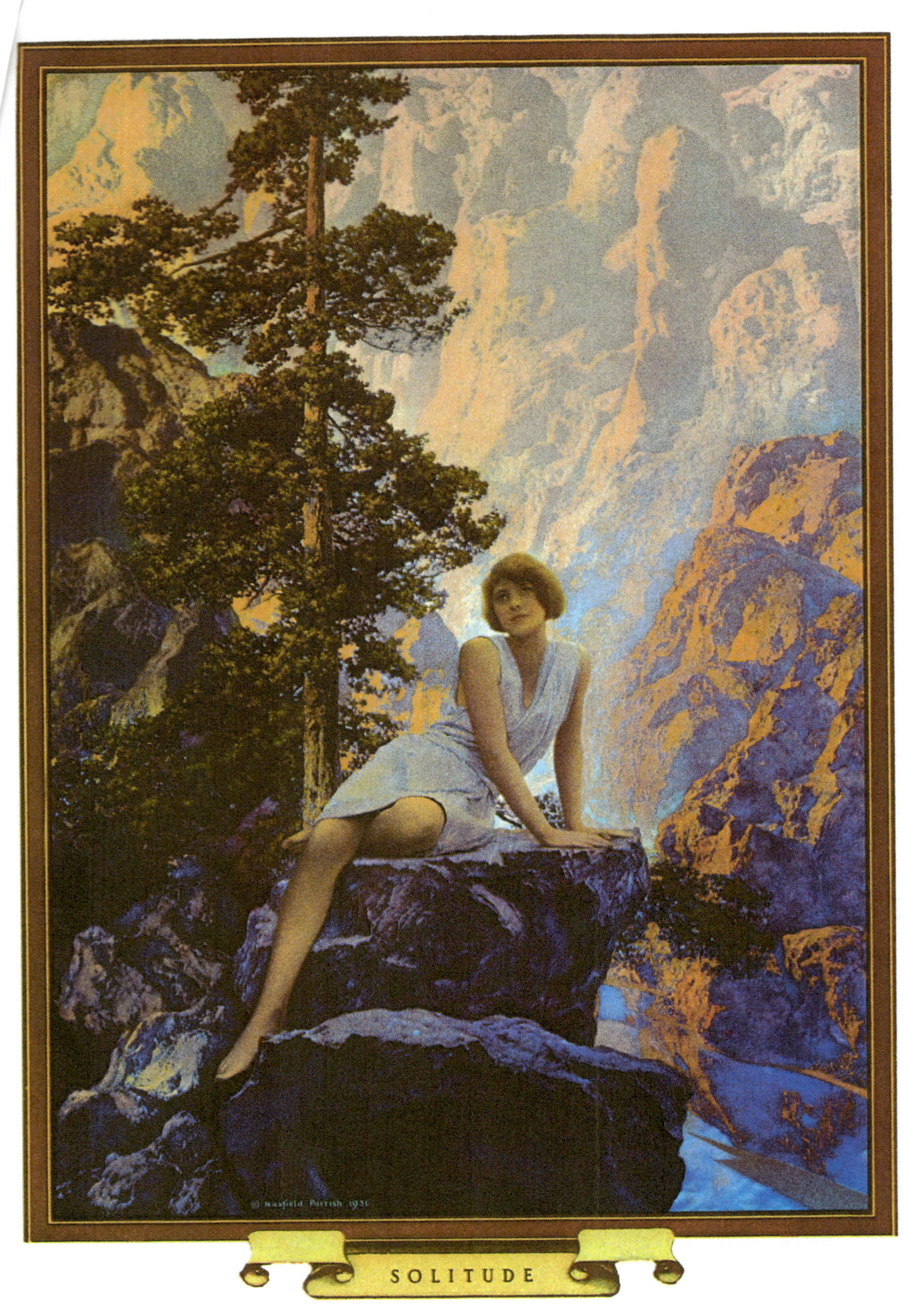

Plate 84.

Solitude

Edison Mazda Lamps calendar, 1932